JEWISH PEDLARS AND HAWKERS

1740-1940

by

BETTY NAGGAR

PORPHYROGENITUS
1992

Porphyrogenitus Ltd.
27/1 Upper Gordon Road,
Camberley, Surrey GU15 2HJ

British Library Cataloguing in Publication Data
Naggar, Betty
Jewish Pedlars and Hawkers, 1740-1940
I. Title
305.5
ISBN 1-871328-05-5

Set by Porphyrogenitus Ltd.
Printed by Lychnos EPE, Athens, Greece.

CONTENTS

1. Private Collection

ACKNOWLEDGEMENTS

I should like to thank the following: American Jewish Committee Library New York, Argyll and Bute District Council Scotland, Bedfordshire County Records Office Bedford, The British Library, The British Museum, The Burrell Collection Glasgow, Central Regional Council Scotland, Cheetham's Library Manchester, Chelmsford County Records Office Essex, City of Birmingham Public Libraries, Dorset County Records Office, Forty Second Street Public Library, Glasgow University Library, G.L.C. Records Office London, Guildhall Library London, Hampshire Records Office Winchester, Hugh Town Museum St. Mary's Isles of Scilly, Inverness Archives Scotland, Jews' College Library London, Jewish Museum London, Kent Archives Office Maidstone, Lerwick Archives Shetland, London School of Economics Library, Luton Hoo Werner Collection; Manchester Central Public Library, Manchester Jewish Museum, Metropolitan Museum New York; Mitchell Library Glasgow, Mocatta Library (now Jewish Studies Library University College London), The National Register of Archives London, The Public Records Office (Chancery Lane & Kew) London, School of Oriental and African Studies University of London, School of Scottish Studies University of Edinburgh, Spanish and Portuguese Synagogue Archives London, Tower Hamlets Public Library, Victoria and Albert Museum Library (Prints); Winchester County Records Office.

I would also like to thank many people for their comments and information, and my daughter who typed and retyped my manuscript. Above all I would like to thank Miss J. Chrysostomides for her constant encouragement, and John Chrysostomides for seeing this book through the press.

2. Guildhall Library and Art Collection

ABBREVIATIONS

ALEXANDER	D. ALEXANDER, *Retailing in England During the Industrial Revolution* (London, 1970).˅
Anglo	*Anglo-Jewish Historical Exhibition Catalogue* (Royal Albert Hall 1887).
ATKINS	R. ATKINS, *A Compendius History of the Israelites* (London, 1810).
AUSTIN	W. AUSTIN, *Letters from London* (Boston, 1802-3).
BEBBINGTON	J. BEBBINGTON, *Autobiography* (MS Solly Collection London School of Economics, 1882).
BENNETT	A.R. BENNETT, *London and Londoners in 1850s and 1860s* (London, 1924).
BERMANT	C. BERMANT, *Point of Arrival* (London, 1975).
BESANT	W. BESANT, *London in the Eighteenth Century* (London, 1902).
BOOTH, *Conditions*	C. BOOTH, *Conditions and Occupations of the People of Tower Hamlets* (London, 1886-1887).
BOOTH, *Life*	C. BOOTH, *Life and Labour of the People of London* (London, 1892).
BOOTH, *Notebooks*	C. BOOTH, *Notebooks 1887* (MS London School of Economics London).
BPP	*British Parliamentary Papers.*
BUSBY	T.L. BUSBY, *Costume of the Lower Orders* (London, 1820).
CHEAP, *History*	J. CHEAP, *The History of John Cheap The Chapman*, Scottish Tracts (Glasgow 1785).
CHESNEY	K. CHESNEY, *The Victorian Underworld* (London, 1970).
Church	*Church and Synagogue* Quarterly Magazine of Parochial and Foreign Mission to the Jews, (London, 1896-1901).

Abbreviations

CLEGG	The Reverend CLEGG, *History and Conversion of Samuel Harris* (Bradford, 1833).
COLERIDGE	S.T. COLERIDGE, *Table Talk* (London, 1884).
COLQUHON	P. COLQUHON, *A Treatise on the Police of the Metropolis* (London, 1797).
D'ARCHENHOLZ	D'ARCHENHOLZ, *Picture of England*, 2v (London, 1789).
DAVIS	D. DAVIS, *A History of Shopping* (London & Toronto, 1966).
DE VEGA	DE VEGA (Pseud.), C. COCHRANE, *Tour Through Great Britain and Ireland* (London, 1828-1829).
DUSHINSKY	C. DUSHINSKY, *The Rabbinate of the Great Synagogue* (Oxford, 1921).
ELM	*The East London Magazine* (London, 1891-1893).
ENDELMAN	T. ENDELMAN, *The Jews of Georgian England* (Philadelphia, 1979).
Eph	*Ephemerides* (British Library).
Everyday	*The Everyday Book* (London, 1827).
Expositor	*The Jewish Expositor* (Monthly), (London, 1819)
FAUCHER	L. FAUCHER, *Etudes sur l'Angleterre* (Paris, 1845).
FELIX	FELIX FOLIO (Pseud.), J. PAGE, *Hawkers and Street Dealers of Manchester* (Manchester, 1858).
GARTNER	L. GARTNER, *The Jewish Immigrant in England 1870-1914* (London, 1960).
Gazette	*The London Gazette* (Weekly) (London, 1744-.).
GEORGE	D. GEORGE, *London Life in the Eighteenth Century* (London, 1925).

6

GM	*The Gentleman's Magazine* (Weekly) (London, 1738-.).
GLRO	Greater London Records Office.
GREENWOOD, *Journeys*	J. GREENWOOD, *Unsentimental Journeys* (London, 1867).
GREENWOOD, *Tramp*	J. GREENWOOD, *On Tramp* (London, 1883).
HARRIS	J. HARRIS, *Random Notes and Reflections* (Liverpool, 1912).
HINDLEY, *Cheap*	C. HINDLEY (Ed.), *Cheap Jack* (London, 1876).
HINDLEY, *Cries*	C. HINDLEY, *The Cries of London* (London, 1881).
HUGHSON	P. HUGHSON (Pseud.), E. PUGH, *Walks Through London* (London, 1817).
Inverness	Inverness Archives.
JACOB	A.M. JACOB, *The Jews of Falmouth* (London, 1949).
Jewish C.	*The Jewish Chronicle* (Weekly) (London).
JHSE	The Jewish Historical Society of England.
JOSEPH	J. JOSEPH, *The History of Petticoat Lane* (London, 1971).
LAROON	M. LARON/LAROON, *Cries of London*, Prints published by Tempest (London, 1688).
Leisure	*Leisure Hour* (Monthly) (London, 1856).
LIPMAN, *Centuries*	V.D.L. LIPMAN, *Three Centuries of Anglo-Jewish History* (London, 1961).
LIPMAN, *Social*	V.D.L. LIPMAN, *Social History of the Jews in England 1850-1950* (London, 1954).
LIPMAN, Origins	V.D.L. LIPMAN, 'Origins of provincial Anglo-Jewry' in *Provincial Jewry in Victorian Britain* (London, 19).
LISSACK	M. LISSACK, *Jewish Perseverance* (Bedford, 1851).

MAINWARING	G. MAINWARING, *Brief Considerations on the Present State of the Police* (London, 1821).
MARGOULIOUTH	M. MARGOULIOUTH, *History of the Jews* (London, 1851).
MAYHEW, *London*	H. MAYHEW, *London Labour and the London Poor* (London, 1861).
MAYHEW, 'Survey'	H. MAYHEW, Survey of London and the Poor (*The Morning Chronicle*, London 1850).
MPP	Metropolitan Police Papers, in PROK under MEP
MILLS	J. MILLS, *The British Jews* (London, 1853).
Mission	School of Oriental and African Studies, Missionary Archives of the Council for World Mission, Mission to the Jews in London (c.1806).
Mocatta	Jewish Studies Library, University College, London.
NATHAN	L. NATHAN, *A Short Account of the Life and Transactions of Levi Nathan* (London, 1776).
OBSP	Old Bailey Session Papers.
OSTERLEY	W.E.O. OSTERLEY, *Walks in Jewry* (London, 1901).
PICCIOTTO	M.H. PICCIOTTO, *Sketches of Anglo-Jewish History* (London, 1875).
PLACE	FRANCIS PLACE *Collection* (London, 1849).
PROCL	Public Records Office, Chancery Lane, London.
PROK	Public Record Office, Kew.
PYNE	W.H. PYNE, *The World in Miniature* (London, 1827).
Repository	*The Jewish Repository* (Magazine of the London Society for promoting Christianity Among the Jews, London 1813-1815).

8

ROTH, *Anglo*	C. ROTH, *Anglo-Jewish Almanacs Jewish Chronicle Supplement* (London, 1936).
ROTH, *Essays*	C. ROTH, *Essays and Portraits in Anglo-Jewish History* (London, 1950).
ROTH, *History*	C. ROTH, *History of the Jews in England* (Oxford, 1941).
ROTH, *Synagogue*	C. ROTH, *History of the Great Synagogue* (London, 1950).
RUBENS	A. RUBENS, *A Jewish Iconography* (London, 1954).
RUMNEY	J. RUMNEY (RUMNAYEK), *The Economic & Social Development of the Jews in England 1730-1860* (Thesis, London University, 1930).
RUSSELL	RUSSELL and LEWIS, *The Jews in London* (London, 1900).
SIMS	G. SIMS, *Off The Track in London* (London, 1907).
SILLIMAN	B. SILLIMAN, *Travels In England, Holland and Scotland* (Boston, Mass., 1805-1806).
SOUTHEY	R. SOUTHEY, *Letters from England* (London 1803-1807).
STALLARD	J.M. STALLARD, *London Pauperism* (London, 1867).
SYDNEY	W.C. SYDNEY, *England in the Eighteenth Century* (London, 1891).
Times	*The Times Newspaper* (London).
TUER	A.W. TUER, *Old London Street Cries* (London, 1887).
WENDEBORN	F.A. WENDEBORN, *View of England* (London, 1791).
WILLIAMS	B. WILLIAMS, *The Making of Manchester Jewry* (Manchester, 1976).
WOLF	L. WOLF, Papers (MS Mocatta Library).

WRIGHT	T. WRIGHT (The Journeyman Engineer), *The Great Unwashed* (London, 1868).
ZANGWILL	I. ZANGWILL, *Children of the Ghetto* (London, 1892).

Jewish Pedlars and Hawkers

Knives Combs or Inkhornes.
Couteaux Peignes Ecritoires.
Calamari Pettini e Coltelli.

Mauron delin:

P. Tempest exc:
CumPrivilegio:

3. Guildhall Library and Art Collection

CHAPTER I

URBAN AND COUNTRY PEDLARS

After the Jews were expelled from England in 1290, there is almost no evidence of their presence until the reign of Queen Elizabeth. In the middle of the 17th century they were readmitted by Cromwell albeit on an understanding rather than officially, and began to form a small community in London. These were Spanish and Portuguese, Sephardic Jews, fleeing the Inquisition. They were "New Christians" known as "Marranos" because they clung to the Jewish faith in secret. Many of them were rich and well educated, though there were a few who were totally destitute on arrival.

Around 1680 a fair number of Dutch and German Jews began to arrive in London and at various seaports. About 1850 and again in 1880 there was an influx of Russian and Polish Jews escaping from increasingly restrictive laws in their countries, as well as from frequent pogroms[1].

A good deal of encouragement to emigrate came from glowing letters from those already established in England and America, telling of the religious and other freedoms and the excellent possibilities for a safer life. The small Sephardic community in England, however, which lived on sufferance and as far as possible out of the public eye, was afraid the arrival of hoards of indigent Jews would reflect badly on them, and particularly that it would be a heavy drain on their resources. The Elders of the community tried to stem the tide with warnings in foreign newspapers[2] and by communications between Rabbis at home and abroad but to little effect. Some immigrants in the 19th century, when the greatest flood occurred, came to England as a staging post on their way to America and decided to stay; others actually thought they had arrived in the U.S.A. and got off the boats in Hull or Glasgow![3]

1. The reasons for their immigration are many, and can be studied elsewhere.
2. BPP, Board of Trade Alien Immigration 1894, p. 5.
3. Mrs. Holston, personal communication.

13

A very few of the immigrants may have had a little money with which they could open shops as small jewellers or watch makers, but the greatest number were absolutely penniless. Owing to the repression under which they had lived, the immigrants were untrained and in England it was not possible for them to enter a number of trades which were ruled by guilds, or to pay the fees required for an apprenticeship. So, as many of them had been pedlars in their own countries, it was natural for them to turn to peddling[4].

The established community, at a loss over what to do with the numbers of poor, and afraid of seeing them begging in the streets, was happy to give a couple of guineas to each poor Sephardic man, to start him off with a pedlar's pack and a few cheap goods or the where withal to start as an old clothes man; and this system was followed in turn by the Askenazis, East European Jews. Sometimes help was given through a system of small loans at interest to be paid on a weekly or monthly basis, which may account for the view that Jews did not beg. Perhaps as a result, it was said that "there is no such thing as a mendicant Jew"[5], "Jews never begged they were merely traders", and "Jews never beg of their own people, a custom highly creditable"[6]. De Vega, in 1828, remarking in conversation on a trait of Jewish character which he said was very prominent, claimed he had never seen a Jew beggar, to which his acquaintance replied "Oh, yes, they do sometimes ... but as soon as they can scrape together a shilling or two, they buy scissors, pencils etc. and if they can get 2d or 3d a day they prefer it to begging"[7]. Occasionally difficult cases were given two guineas on the understanding they would leave the country and not come back for two years[8], as was the case with Jacob Cardoso who was sent to Holland[9]. Reading between the lines this is what may

---

4. ENDELMAN, p. 176.
5. ENDELMAN, p. 176; *Leisure*, July 1856, p. 497
6. T.T. SMITH, *Vagabondia*, (London, 1817).
7. DE VEGA, vol. I, p. 78.
8. GEORGE, p. 127.
9. RUMNEY

also have happened to Levi Nathan, an old clothes man. Having lost his job, his home, his money, and his wife and children having left him, all due to the pursuit of the scheming Mrs. Parry (who later quit him for another man), he left for France. He was given "a few guineas into my snuff box" and he went by coach to Brighthelmstow from an inn in Wood Street[10]. However, he was soon back; and many other pedlars used to journey to England five or six times a year, to buy old clothes, as Henry Simons did on his unfortunate visit[11].

There were still English pedlars, and according to one author more non-Jewish than Jewish ones. In *Cheap Jack*'s biography (1876) there are only occasional references to foreign pedlars and in John Bebbington's (1882) none at all. In the Hawkers' & Pedlars' Office accounts from 1707 to 1714 only five recognizable Jewish names (Isaac Dias, Chaim Leonard, Isaac Lewis, Emmanuel Enriques and Isaac Polack) occur amongst well over one hundred licences[12].

But as time went on more and more immigrants arrived and the word *pedlar* or *hawker* became almost synonymous with *Jew*. So much so that in 1828 a cultured Jew in Scotland said that he was mortified to be taken for a packman, and being asked to sell a razor or a knife[13]. This development is evidenced by the many sometimes cruel caricatures depicting them. In the earlier prints of the *Cries of London* they appear to be like the other criers, but later they take on exaggerated Jewish characteristics. The Old Clothes men were all said to be Jews.

The Jewish community did establish some form of organization for helping the Jewish poor, though it was not particularly effective. An article in 1903 remarks on the admirably managed Jewish charities providing for the poor's needs, but that was over one hundred and fifty years after the first immigrants arrived. In any case the Board

10. NATHAN, p. 30.
11. See below 37.
12. PROCL, E.351/1738, E.351/1739.
13. *The Jew Exile* (London, 1828), vol. I, p. 10.

15

2

of Guardians (who looked after the Jewish poor) did not generally help the immigrants until they had been six months in England. Some, who decided to return to their countries were said to receive a certain sum from them at the last moment of departure "in order that the poor creatures on their arrival may not be entirely destitute"[14]. Social attitudes of the time may explain the following passage, "How far these institutions act as a magnet for the Russian Pale and the ghettoes of Poland must be an open question — all charity tends to create poverty as well as cure it"[15].

However, the communities were at pains to prevent immigrant Jews becoming a burden on the country. In a Select Committee Report on Alien Immigration (1888) Sir Samuel Hoare was asked "Can you speak within your knowledge of any instance of their (e.g. Jewish immigrants) being in any way supported by the rates, either indoor or outdoor relief?", to which the answer was "No, I do not know of a single case"[16]. A clergyman remarked that their habits of industry, and the help given by national charities precluded extreme want or misery[17]; and an historian and social observer also commented on their independence and that they only applied for relief in case of extreme distress[18].

Until the arrival of cheap, new, ready made garments made possible by the invention of the sewing machine and by *sweated* labour (a system which broke tailoring work down into separate parts i.e. button holer, liner, sleeve setter etc., instead of one man for each suit), there was, for the poor, no alternative to second-hand clothing, though most poor people despised it[19]. Thus, the old clothes man formed an integral part of the economy, though working almost exclusively in London and a few large cities. The urban pedlars on the

---

14. STALLARD, pp. 5-7.
15. 'Alien Immigrant' in *Blackwoods Magazine* (Edinburgh, 1903), p. 106.
16. BPP, Select Committee Report, Alien Immigration 1888.
17. MILLS, p. 257.
18. J. HOLLINGSHEAD, *Ragged London* (London, 1861), p. 48.
19. CHESNEY, pp. 191-2.

contrary, were only adjunct to the ordinary shops, supposedly, and certainly in the eyes of the public, cheaper, though in reality their goods were more often than not of a lower quality. Their usefulness was limited, unlike the country pedlars who were an important factor in the distributive system. Later, in the 19th century, urban pedlars served as a liaison between shops and suburbs where no shops yet existed[20].

Both urban and country pedlars, old clothes hawkers and also shopkeepers, had different roles in the economy, but their trades were not exclusive, all of them being interchangeable. Levi Nathan, old clothes man, became a country pedlar and went to France[21]; and Isaac Ashur said "Sometimes I am an old clothes man, and sometimes I travel the country with hardware"[22]. Again, some country pedlars, as well as their usual goods, carried second-hand clothes, and pedlars in the Isles of Scilly up to 1948 used to take orders for suits made to measure and brought them next time they came round[23]. Urban pedlars, too, occasionally went "on the tramp" and walked into the country, and some of them had regular 39 mile walks out to the suburbs. One wily fellow often went into the country when he noticed country pedlars coming into London, thus seizing an empty market[24].

Some country pedlars moved into the towns in winter when the roads became impassable, renting a room in which to display their wares, thus for all intents and purposes, becoming shop keepers. This was known as a *bazaar*, but by 1889 had fallen out of favour as it became difficult to find a shop or room to let for a short time, and also the regular shops now sold the type of goods formerly only to be

20. ALEXANDER, p. 233.
21. NATHAN, p. 30.
22. OBSP, 1781-1782, p. 272.
23. Mr. Trenear (age 91), personal communication.
24. SIMS, *Living London* (London, 1904-6), vol. II, p. 318; MAYHEW, *London*, vol. I, p. 379.

found in the bazaars[25]. The custom lingered on in the remoter parts of Britain. A seller and mender of watches and clocks hired a shop for two weeks every year in St. Mary's Scilly, circa 1930, and a pedlar (Mr. Phillips) hired a hall for a week on the tiny island of Bryher every summer, circa 1920, to sell various goods, but mostly toys[26]. Shop keepers in their turn often had to take to hawking during slack periods[27], as did costers when it became impossible to sell fruit during a cholera epidemic[28].

So it can be seen that there was a general fluidity between the various trades. All these moves are exemplified in the life of John Bebbington, whose autobiography, beautifully written on pieces of notepaper, describes how he went from costermongering to peddling, to shop keeping, and back again to peddling in town and country, with an interval of some years in an indoor job, probably clerking. This interesting, partially self-educated man, whose ethical ideas for the betterment of the poor were of an original nature for that time, seems at his happiest when walking the countryside as a pedlar.

The Jewish country pedlars led a very different life from the urban pedlars or the clothes men. They had to combat loneliness, incomprehension, hard grinding work, bad weather, illness, and what was worse, the real danger of robbery or even murder. It is extraordinary how these often physically small men, most of whom had little or no knowledge of English, had the courage to tramp their way around the countryside.

Often there was no possibility of a clean, or indeed of any, bed at night, or any bite to eat, during the day, except bread, butter and tea. Unable to chat to a friend or neighbour, they were

25. HINDLEY, *Cheap*, p. 107; ALEXANDER, p. 79.
26. Mrs. Stedeford (St. Mary's, Isles of Scilly), personal communication.
27. Abraham de Silva, who was a confectioner, said that at one part of the year when his business was dead, he became a dealer and chapman, i.e. pedlar: OBSP, 1798-1799, p. 651; BPP, Board of Trade, Alien Immigration 1894, LXXIII, p. 63.
28. BEBBINGTON, f. J. 348.

obliged to buy and sell and make a living for themselves and their families. Even the English pedlars found life hard and gains few, as can be seen by the many pedlars' and chapmens' bankruptcies posted in the *Gentleman's Magazine* and the *London Gazette*[29]. As Wright, the author of *Tramps & Tramping*, said, "it is a terrible life"[30]. Samuel Harris, an immigrant, said "I was a stranger in a strange land and had only sixpence in my pocket with little prospect of taking any money that day"[31], and Joel Rabbinovitz described how "the pedlar trudges from town to town and city to city staggering under his burden. He is parched in Summer and frozen in Winter and his eyes wither in their sockets before he gets a sight of a coin"[32]. An old trader who sold barometers in the mountainous parts of Cumbria, and later turned to selling old clothes, mentioned the loneliness of walking sometimes for hours without seeing anyone[33]. And when they first started their trade the pedlars were often away from home for many months at a time, returning perhaps, in winter when the weather made life impossible on the roads. In some remote villages in the 18th century, strangers were so rare that they were viewed with curiosity and occasionally the dogs were set on them[34].

In 'The Traveller', a short story by Zangwill, he explained the solitude and fears of a Jewish hawker. How, when he entered a pub he was chaffed and gibed at in a language of which he understood only the cruelty — he was "a footsore mendicant buffeted and reviled"[35].

29. *Gazette*, March 1st 1739, April 12th 1739, 1744, etc.
30. WRIGHT, p. 258.
31. CLEGG, p. 24.
32. GARTNER, p. 59.
33. MAYHEW, *London*, vol. II, p. 122.
34. SYDNEY, vol. II, p. 218.
35. ZANGWILL, *The Traveller*, pp. 11-2 (Box pamphlets, The Mocatta Library).

This treatment was in sharp contrast to the welcome a pedlar received in earlier times. Then, he was welcomed as the bringer of news and the story teller in the evening round the fire. He was rewarded with what was known as *the Pedlars' Draught*, and would often be given a bed for the night, paying for it with little bits and fancy pieces from his pack, though this idealised view is contradicted by a pedlar's autobiography[36].

Sending the immigrants into the country appears to have been a deliberate strategy on the part of the Community's elders. In 1897 Dr. Adler, Chief Rabbi, interviewed by Charles Booth, said that the leaders of the congregation were anxious to "diffuse" the newcomers, as they became Anglicized more quickly in the countryside[37].

A missionary, the Rev. John Knight, thought some travelling Jews pretended to be Christians. This however seems at first unlikely and judging by a letter from him to Robert Winter, another missionary, was probably a misunderstanding. Rev. Knight wrote asking about a Mrs. Cohen, who had come to his house one evening and begged him to find her lodgings for the night. He recommended a house in the village, and on arrival she asked for food, saying she would pay next day as she had left laces and shawls at Mr. Knights'. When she was found to be lying they turned her away and she left saying she had friends in the next village. Mr. Knight writes if she is not Mrs. Cohen, whom he knew to be a baptized Jewess, they must warn people of her as an imposter[38].

The distances the pedlars covered, usually on foot, at least until they had saved some money, were astonishing, particularly as they were carrying heavy packs. Some went from Fair to Fair in different towns, others circled round one town or county, others again seem to have moved through chance meetings on the road or simply because they thought a place might be good for work. Already in

---

36. CHEAP, *History*.
37. BOOTH, *Notebooks*, XXVII, B 196/202.
38. Mission, Letter dated 24 Dec. 1806.

1742, a Jewish pedlar, Samuel Emmanuel, had reached Morpeth in Northumberland. He was being pursued for debt, but disappeared abroad[39]. And hearsay states there was a Russian Jewish pedlar in Lerwick, Shetland before 1846[40].

There is a fascinating short autobiography of a pedlar's round, written by John Cheap in 1785. He got his name "by selling twenty needles for a penny and two leather laces for a farthing". His business was basically buying and selling brass pots, which he liked "heavy", and human hair. He even cut the latter from the owners' heads when they sold it to him! He described his stays in various farms and tells of the difficulties in getting a bed for the night, with the result that he often ended up in a barn. On one occasion he spent the night sitting up near the fire, because some Scottish drovers threatened to kill him if he didn't give up his bed; and on another he had to sleep in a pigsty, where the sow attacked him in the middle of the night to defend her seven piglets. Farmers seemed wary of him, and John says one farmer complains that chapmen come seeking a room, but when later on they grow rich and have a shop, are too proud to let people peer in the windows. He also found it hard to get food, even when he offered to pay for it, except towards evening when the farmers' wives would, to get rid of him quickly, give him a pot of cabbage or a cake. One man told John his minister preached against giving food to beggars, but he did relent and sold John his own supper for 2d.

Although John's story contains a good deal of coarse, salacious humour, he does not attempt to hide the underlying harshness of a hawker's life, and his testimony confirms the various points made by other travellers. It is possible that this story is part of folk-lore, as

39. *Gazette*, no. 8333, June 1774.
40. Other evidence states his arrival was in 1908: Mrs. Hofman, personal communication.

various editions of it appear in Glasgow and Edinburgh — but even if it is, it is certainly based on fact, not fancy[41].

Another pedlar, "Old Sammy" an aged Jew, walked seventy-two miles from London to Free Market fair in Portsmouth, and was said to have walked this route once a year for fifty years. When he arrived he always stood in the same place[42]. Cheap Jack mentioned quite casually that he himself walked from Birmingham to Portsea.

Samuel Harris (circa 1820) arrived in Gravesend from Germany, and just taking time to pick up some money from a collection made for him by the Jews of Dukes Place, London, bought some goods, and set off as a pedlar. He must have been a strange sight because he was laughed at for his foreign clothes. He walked twenty miles the first day, and three weeks later reached Birmingham where he continued in and around the town for some months. He then went to Bristol, but as business was bad, he set off for Bridgewater, Taunton and Exeter, and further travelled in Devon and Cornwall. After returning to Birmingham, he went on to Warwickshire and fairs in Staffordshire. Meeting two friends, he decided to make for Newcastle Fair and "set off about two o'clock on Sunday with the intention to walk all that night as it was forty-two miles distant, and we wished to be there at the commencement of the fair. We arrived the next morning in good time"! From there he went to Manchester, Newcastle, back to Manchester, Stafford and Liverpool. And this on really appalling roads which people at that time were always complaining of. In the 18th century roads were in such bad condition and were otherwise so dangerous that travellers sometimes wrote their wills before setting off. Pedlars called good main roads *High Spice Toby*.

Samuel was obviously a born traveller as he later decided to go to Poland to visit his parents — but ended up in Copenhagen and returned to Liverpool[43]. As though that was not

41. CHEAP, *History*
42. HINDLEY, *Cheap*, p. 183.
43. CLEGG, pp. 23-4, 36, 76.

enough, he took a further trip as steward on a boat going to Sierra Leone.

Interestingly, whenever he fell on bad times, the local Jewish Community, wherever he happened to be, came to his aid. On one occasion he was given seven shillings from the Jewish Poor Strangers' Fund which must have been used to calls on its charity from wandering pedlars. This may have been a revival or continuance of an 11th century custom, whereby poor Jewish travellers, particularly scholars, were often supported by local communities[44].

Joseph Harris (no relation) circa 1860 but writing in 1902, had a much more regular round. He started off walking twenty eight miles to Beverly, and then took a train to Hull and thence to Whitby. He always returned to the same place at regular intervals, thus he was sure of a bed and was able to leave a dirty shirt and socks to be washed by accommodating landladies, to await his next visit[45]. This was an excellent idea, as one pedlar complained he had to walk about in the sun to dry his wet clothes which were soaking from the day before, as "there is no means in these places to dry them"[46]. Joseph always stayed at home on Saturdays and cleaned his stock on Sundays.

Solomon Nathan, indicted for breaking and entering and stealing Elkan Hymen the silk-weaver's goods, attempted the perfect alibi by detailing his round as follows: "I went with Edward Porter (taking handkerchiefs, ribbons and lace) on Monday 2nd and 3rd of March to Hitchin, Herts — we slept there Monday evening, attended the market Tuesday; left Hitchin Tuesday evening, went to Dunstable, attended the market Wednesday, slept there Wednesday and Thursday night and left on Friday morning for St. Albans. Slept there Saturday and Sunday and returned to London on Monday"[47].

44. S.D. GOITEIN, *A Mediterranean Society* (Los Angeles, 1971), pp. 95-6.
45. HARRIS, p. 23.
46. BEBBINGTON, Folio J. 382.
47. OBSP, 1833-1834, p. 604.

One man went regularly from Liverpool to South Wales and back, selling and replenishing his stock en route; but he did have a pony and trap. He was known as Welsh Harry[48]. In Scotland, pedlars travelled from Glasgow to the villages in Ayr and Lanark, and from Edinburgh to Fife and from Falkirk to Stirlingshire[49]. It was also in Scotland that three pedlars aged seventeen, fourteen and "age unknown", and two friends walked from Glasgow to Inverness via Inverary in 1825. From that base, staying in "the Shetland woman's house", they travelled to Cambeltown, Fort George and the Black Isle. They were later accused of stealing quite an unlikely quantity of goods from a shop, and were taken to the "police office". There, young Macrae who had sold them the goods "lifted up a box from under the counter", whatever that may imply. Further confusion arose because Macrae said he was unable to identify the goods sold by his son, and also because one pedlar was carrying another pedlar's goods as his friend had no room in his own box. They were put on trial in spite of the lack of evidence, and one pedlar even had a list of his goods which tallied with what was found in his box. The outcome is unknown.[50]

A Russian Jewish pedlar arrived in the Shetlands c.1900. He was said to have been "a cossack" — "which you would believe if you had seen him ride"- and to have escaped from Russia to avoid being forced into the army, (Jewish conscripts had to serve 12 years in the most terrible situations and very rarely survived). Another pedlar and later his son, travelled about the islands by bicycle and boat selling jewellery and old clothes, and is still remembered by the local inhabitants who were always happy to invite him to a meal and give him a bed for the night[51].

---

48. Albert Feather, personal communication.

49. ed. K. COLLINS, *Aspects of Scottish Jewry* (Glasgow, 1987).

50. Inverness, L/INV/BC 14/98A.

51. Mrs. E.G. Hofman, personal communication. Another Russian Jewish pedlar sold gold watches in the islands of the Inner Hebrides up till 1940. He came from Glasgow and used to bring pit ponies to the island of Gigha to pasture. He told the local inhabitants he had walked from Russia! Yet another

John Bebbington's round was generally based on the various fairs and market days. He went from London to Birmingham[52], which was a favourite stop for pedlars, as they could buy cheap goods which were manufactured there[53], then to Derby Market and Nottingham Goose Fair, where he stayed for a week. After that he went to Manchester and Woodhead, eighteen miles in a day, and he also speaks of a walk of fourteen or fifteen miles on a very windy day. John loved the countryside, and there is in his autobiography a striking picture of Yorkshire:

> "The Old Woman's house (where he was to stay in the attic one very stormy night) was built on the edge of a deep ravine, one of the particularities of Yorkshire: you will find on one side of the roadhills towering above your head, on the other deep dells or valleys which a sudden thrust would hurl the traveller in such depth in all probability he would never live to tell how he fell. I noticed a railway station so far below me that it appeared no longer than a shed. On the side of the ravine the hills rose to a considerable height, thickly clothed with trees and several large waterfalls pouring

pedlar, McAlister, actually rowed across from the mainland to the 'Inner Islands'. The distance to Gigha from the mainland, which now takes 20 minutes by ferry, must have been a long row. Miss McNeil personal communication.

52. BEBBINGTON, f. J. 381.
53. MARGOULIOUTH, vol. III, p. 105.

down the hillside with considerable noise"[54].

Wright (circa 1868) who was a seasoned tramping character, sometimes walked forty or fifty miles in a day and thought nothing of twenty-eight miles distance. He remarked that "I resolved that I would that day do the larger half of sixty-five miles that still lay between me and London"!

He says in his autobiography that working men did not despise tramps but thought of them as a working man on the road in quest of work and travelling on foot because they had no money. He gives much useful information for travellers, such as, never accept old boots as they are too uncomfortable; the best pair of boots were strong lace-ups which have never been cobbled, and were well greased. He provides many cheap recipes for the manufacture of Dubbin, which softened the leather and kept out damp. Where there was dry grass it was better to walk without shoes and whenever possible feet should be washed every day — leaving them dirty, contrary to old wives' wisdom did not, he says, harden them. He thought that it was better to travel by night in summer and sleep by day, and that it was good for two to walk together for company. An experienced tramp, according to Wright, knew who would give lifts, or a drink of milk, and he always carried a tool kit to repair public house machinery. He knew too, how to tell what the weather would do, what roads to take, and how to spend money on cheap food. But sometimes, he added you could find fruit and vegetables between towns! Nevertheless he must have known hunger for he once chided a man who threw away a piece of bread in these terms, "the day will come when thou'll be glad on a bit o' bread like that you've chucked away. When you're on t'road you'll think turnips good eating and look on bread as Sunday Grub"[55].

54. BEBBINGTON, f. J. 382.
55. WRIGHT, p. 27ff.

Cheap Jack, who travelled twenty miles in a morning, went on Wednesday to Romford Market, Thursday to Bishop Stortford, Friday to Chelmsford, and Saturday to Colchester; Monday to Hadleigh, Wednesday to Bury St. Edmunds, Thursday to Diss and on Saturday to Norwich. However, he rather disdained pedlars who walked, and said a Cheap Jack had to have £100 worth of paid up goods, a good horse and carriage or he was thought nothing of. He spoke of a man who had a large stock of goods and a double carriage, that is, one end for business, the other for living and sleeping in[56]. He himself had a cart, but when his horse lamed, bought a light cart and two dogs to pull it. He covered one hundred and forty miles in seven days and then exchanged the dogs (probably worn out, poor things) for a donkey, known in the trade as a Jerusalem pony[57].

Dogs were much used for travelling and could go very far and fast. It was said a pair of good dogs could go as fast as a horse and chaise, at least for some miles. One man had a kind of vehicle pulled by four dogs with which he used to drive regularly between London and Brighton, keeping up with fast coaches for many a mile without the dogs jibbing[58].

According to Cheap Jack, with a light load, say about two hundredweight, a couple of well-bred dogs and a properly built cart, "a person could run around England in no time — and then the turn-out is so very inexpensive"[59]. Dogs had an advantage, for they were not counted for licensing[60], though at one time dogs were only allowed to pull carts once they were twelve miles outside London, so

---

56. HINDLEY, *Cheap*, pp. 1-10.
57. Ibid., p. 140.
58. FELIX, p. 25.
59. HINDLEY, *Cheap*, p. 141.
60. PROK, IR51, p. 174.

they ran free, the pedlar pulling the cart, till they reached the twelve-mile stone, when they were harnessed up[61].

After the Act against using dogs as draught animals became law c.1846, many hawkers put handles on their barrows and pulled them themselves, or replaced dogs with donkeys. Some men had a horse or donkey without a barrow or cart — the horse carrying the stock and the pedlar walking. There is a 19th century print of a pedlar leading a horse which has a large trunk and a basket on its back, the usual box hanging round the man's neck[62]. A pedlar, who made and sold brooms, mended shoes and could tailor a little, told De Vega that if he didn't succeed in one town, he went elsewhere and generally managed to find something to do; "we walk ourselves but our furniture and stock is carried by our donkey"[63].

An unusual form of travel was undertaken by Barnet Levy (whose original name was Bernard Beer, as explained in J. Solomon's letter to Lucien Wolf) and his newly wed wife. Unable to make a living as a soap boiler in London, Barnet decided to become a pedlar and go to Cornwall. His wife, Esther, who had a good English education and was "a delicate and refined lady" did not fancy travelling "pell mell" in Russel Foley's wagon to get there. This was an immense vehicle with a canvas roof and straw on the floor, the entrance into which was via a ladder, the traveller tumbling from it onto the straw beneath the tilt. It was pulled by six horses and had an armed guard on a pony to protect the passengers from highway men[64]. Something of the type is mentioned by a French voyager in 1719, who lists three types of coach; the expensive stage coaches

---

61. HINDLEY, *Cheap*, p. 141. The two travelling *barrow men* who were tried at York for robbery and murder, each owned a vehicle drawn by dogs. But Mayhew says few itinerants had animals to pull their carts, this perhaps because he wrote mostly about London pedlars. In fact the number of licences for horses increased steadily. See below 125.

62. DAVIS, p. 14, illustration.

63. DE VEGA, vol. I, p. 314.

64. See note 68.

going to all important towns; the "flying" coach which could travel 20 leagues in a day but did not go everywhere; and great covered-in carts which lumbered along at a snail's pace, but were patronized because they were cheap[65]. Travelling was expensive, for instance a post shay and four from Holyhead to Bangor, 25 miles, in 1775 cost eight guineas for two people and nine for three[66]; so Barnet hired a pack horse and Esther rode behind him[67].

The journey was three hundred miles and took some days. Each night they stayed in the village or town inn, which was frequented by Jews. The journey was the more extraordinary when the state of the roads is taken into account. In 1742 commenting on this very road, a traveller remarked that as it was a long journey, and there was need for a good road from the West, that was what he expected to find. On the contrary, after the first forty-seven miles he never set eyes on a turnpike (i.e. a well-built, well maintained road) for the two hundred and twenty remaining miles. The various parishes, he said, could or would do nothing about it, and the inhabitants had not the ability to make or mend a road, however much money was given them to do so[68].

The question of lodgings, health and weather, all interacting, were of particular importance to the country pedlars. Lodgings on Friday nights and Saturdays, were in many cases, provided for. It is well known that the Jewish pedlars would meet on a Friday evening, in some inn where a special cupboard was kept for their dishes, which after they had been washed up, were chalked with Hebrew letters to prevent their use — (non-Kosher) — during their

65. SYDNEY, vol. II, p. 15.

66. Reverend Dr. CAMBELL, *Diary of a Visit to England* (Sydney, 1775), p. 15.

67. WOLF, B29. See note 70.

68. *GM*, 1752, p. 519. Parishes had surveyors of roads who were called to attend meetings with Justices of the Peace, to report on their state and expenses.

absences. (I once saw a dish in a Danish country museum with a Star of David scratched on the bottom). One of the pedlars would arrive early on Friday morning to slaughter the chickens to prepare the meal — he would receive one day's estimated profit on his business to compensate him. Sometimes they would meet in the house or shop of one of their brethren who had advanced in business life[69].

One such, Zender Falmouth, who was originally known as Henry Moses, had a jewellery business; and hawkers would gather on a Friday at his large brick house (at that time considered quite a luxury)[70]. They ate together and said prayers on Saturday (ten men being required for a prayer meeting) and on Sunday they would make up their accounts, pay back loans, and be furnished with more goods for their packs.

Zender also paid for some of their licences, but only if the hawker agreed to change his original name to an English Jewish one, which then became his family name[71]. Later, it has been

---

69. ROTH, *Essays*, p. 133.

70. L. FAUCHER, *Manchester in 1844* (Manchester, 1844), p. 11.

71. WOLF, B29 (Provincial Jewries). In a letter to Lucien Wolf, dated 23rd August 1885: *History of the Jewish residents in Cornwall from the early part of the year 1770* by J. Solomon, New York; the first settlers in Cornwall about this date were foreigners generally hawkers carrying on their backs a very heavy loaded box called a marsh the term Marsh was a German patois name for Buckle an article used very extensively by both sexes on shoes and other portions of clothing. ... Henry Moses known as Zender Falmouth with Benjamin Wolf founded the first congregation. ... Moses became a man of substance built himself a large brick house in which he resided and supplied hawkers with goods, to some of them he accorded credit on condition to return every Friday to Falmouth early enough to form one of the congregation, and on the Sunday morning, settle the account, furnish themselves with what goods was required for the coming weeks and also in some instances he advanced the money to purchase a licence for hawking, but always obliged the hawker to have a full Jewish name inserted in the licence and the name introduced in place of the original name became ever after the Family name. The two of the writers' grandfathers' family names were

suggested, he might introduce them to suitable young girls to marry. As the pedlar saved money, he would buy a shop, probably a jeweller's or silver-smiths, and in his turn employ pedlars to sell his goods in the country. In this way, small Jewish communities grew up all over England and Scotland.

By 1740, probably the first series of lodging houses which catered for Jews had spread across the country, where the travellers met in a kind of club, or brotherhood, but by 1830 these clubs had disappeared. Nevertheless, something of the brotherhood remained, as pedlars always knew each other's whereabouts[72]. Other provision might be made by local families. In Sheffield in the 1820's there was only one Jewish family, but on Fridays the mother told the children to look out for Jewish travellers, and bring them home, and as a result they were never without the required number for a service on Saturday[73].

In 1750 there must have been very few Jewish families in Liverpool — for every Friday messages were sent out to the Jewish lodging houses in Chester, Newton, Parkgate etc. to invite the pedlars for an evening meal to be sure to make up a congregation for Saturday's service [74]. These rare evenings and days in the warmth of family life, must have meant much to men who were spending months away from wife and children "in a solitude alleviated only by a Sabbath in a Synagogue town"[75].

On the road, decent lodgings were often hard, or impossible to come by. One old rhubarb trader said he always stayed in public houses rather than lodgings, because he could sell his spices to the proprietors. "I liked it then," he said, "for I was young and

replaced as follows one name was Israel Behrends replaced and called Israel Solomon, the other, Bernard Beer to Barnet Levy.

72. WILLIAMS, p. 2.
73. GARTNER, *The Old and the New in provincial Jewries* p. 29.
74. MARGOULIOUTH, vol. III, p. 110.
75. ZANGWILL, p. 2.

strong and didn't care to sleep twice in the same town"[76]. Cheap Jack liked to sleep out in the summer, lying under his cart by the side of the road, but his friend, Old Sammy, who wasn't used to it, kept banging his head against the bolts and springs of the axle-tree; he also found it too cold[77].

In the 19th century, tramps who were members of a traveller's society had a route book which enabled them to lodge at night, and also receive 18p per day when they were on the road. They also had frequent free meals from members. This was known as "working the ticket"[78].

Many foreigners had difficulty being accepted as lodgers, as one pub-owner remarked to De Vega, "there are too many of these 'ere Jews and Italians about the country"[79]. And Simons was refused a room for the same reason: "I was by," a witness said in court, "when the Jew applied to Mr. Rickets for lodging. Mr Rickets denied him, he asked again and pulled out money, I think it was sixpence and said 'I have money to pay'". Mr. Rickets said "you are the wrong country, I can't lodge you"[80]. And on another occasion he had to open his shirt to show he was clean before he could get a bed[81].

Samuel Harris on the first night of his travels had not enough money for lodgings and anyhow he didn't know how to ask for them, so he passed the night in a field. He must have been a peculiar sight standing in a field saying his morning prayers. Not surprisingly, a stranger came up to ask what his phylacteries were for.

76. MAYHEW, *London*, vol. I, p. 122.
77. HINDLEY, *Cheap*, p. 16.
78. GREENWOOD *Tramp*, p. 39.
79. DE VEGA, vol. II, p. 388.
80. OBSP, 1755, p. 153.
81. OBSP, 1755, p. 154. As late as 1920 Indian traders who visited the Isles of Scilly, never came round in the summer, as lodgings were impossible to get at that time owing to summer visitors, at least this was the reason given by Mrs Thomas in a personal communication.

Samuel replied, "Me no Englishman", which closed the conversation. But he later sold his interlocutor something for 3s[82].

Joseph Harris (no relation) also spoke no English, and was taught to say, "Will you buy"? and hold up his fingers to show the price. He paid 3s. and 6d. for a bed for the night, and lived on bread, butter, tea and sugar[83]. Elkan Solomon, who was a traveller and licensed hawker accepted one of his countryman's offer to walk with him as interpreter as he knew no English. He was to share all profits, although the goods were Elkan's, and the partnership foundered when Elkan accused his companion of stealing seven pairs of earrings value 25s, two brooches value 5s, and his box, value 2s[84].

John Bebbington too, though English, and not a Jew, describes the difficulties of getting a bed for the night. Because of their trade, pedlars had to stay in, or near, towns where there were fairs or market days, and consequently few empty rooms to spare in the pubs and lodging houses. He preferred furnished lodgings and thought them better than pubs or common lodging houses; approaching a reluctant landlady he was asked if he wanted a whole, or half a bed. On offering the extra money for a whole one, and a week's pay in advance, she agreed to take him, and even then he found two working mill girls sharing his room. He mentions handing over his box to his landlady but does not say if this was a safety precaution or an earnest of his honesty. On another occasion he came to a village where there were only two pubs, both completely full up owing to a hiring fair in the neighbourhood, so he trudged on for three miles to the next village, only to find the same situation. "I offered three shillings to be in the stable, or hay loft or anywhere, but every place was full, and the next village four miles away". John then tried, unsuccessfully, to make a hole in a haystack, and finished up in a barn[85].

82. CLEGG, p. 24.
83. HARRIS, p. 23.
84. OBSP, 1847-1848, p. 519.
85. BEBBINGTON, f. J. 381, p. 34; J. 404, p. 57; J. 405, p. 58; J. 377, p. 30.

Sleeping in empty buildings seems to have been quite normal. John Bebbington's first thought on reaching a town was to look for something of this kind. One night, for example, he found a large empty warehouse, where he slept. Another pedlar slept under the shambles in the Fleet market[86]. This was however considered an offence. In 1821 two men were arrested, though later released, for sleeping on the pens after Bartholomew Fair[87].

The importance of the weather to the pedlars, for both earnings and health, cannot be overestimated. Insufficiently covered against the rain and frequently having to sleep out of doors and/or in wet clothes, it is not surprising to find that many of them fell ill. T. Wright, experienced though he was, could not always avoid the bad weather, and tells of a day when he had only walked seven miles before the rain drenched him, followed by a cold wind which made his clothes cling to him. He was only saved from the resulting fever, by a kind landlady who nursed him[88].

John Bebbington was often ill, and had to give up a thriving business on one occasion because of it. He remarks on the weather many times, "on a very windy day", "a dark cold night with heavy clouds threatening rain", "awoke one morning to find the wind at rest and the sky almost without a cloud, and stirring out of bed pulled on my clothes almost as wet as I pulled them off the night before"; "one of the stormiest summers I ever remember, Fair after Fair, Market after Market did I stand in during the whole day, in the drenching rain soaked to the skin without taking a single penny"[89]. Another comment comparing shop-owners and hawkers, says that the latter have to travel with a heavy load many miles a day under a burning sun, or to sit at a stall all day enduring the bitter blast of winter to get saturated by the driving storm[90].

86. OBSP, 1816-1817, p. 41.
87. PLACE, vol. 49, p. 250.
88. WRIGHT, p. 273.
89. BEBBINGTON, f. J. 377, p. 30.
90. FELIX, p. 14.

Samuel Harris too, often fell ill, and once, when he was in hospital the local Jews brought him food three times a day, or he would have eaten nothing but dry bread. Another time he was so ill he couldn't trade, and had to sell off his whole stock at half price to other pedlars[91].

George Gerson, a Russian Jew aged thirty nine, who came to England as an interpreter, was even more unlucky. He married, had four children, and decided he would earn more as a pedlar. In the course of his work he caught a cold which brought on "expectoration", and he died ten months later of a "decline"[92]. John Stallard who had been a hawker since childhood said he suffered with rheumatism "and had a dreadful bad leg"[93].

The weather influenced both the takings and the number of months the men could work profitably. De Vega remarked that the rain had a bad effect on all travellers' gains[94]; and John Bebbington, after an excellent time selling till eleven o'clock at night, without even stopping to eat or drink, awoke to find the ground covered with snow a foot deep, and continuing to fall all day. So he didn't earn a penny, and cut short his travels and instead of visiting several other fairs, decided to go home to London[95]. One old rhubarb and spice seller sums it up, "When dere is bad weather I have de rheumatics oh! very bad, sometimes I can hardly stand or walk"[96].

But greater than the danger of variable weather or sudden illness was the ever present one of robbery and sometimes murder. The hawkers were, of course, known to carry money and/or goods which were more or less valuable, and so were a tempting target for evil-doers. They were, too, often robbed of their licences. Cheap

91. CLEGG, p. 44.
92. *Expositor*, vol. IV, p. 477.
93. PROK, IR51.5 1832, p. 12.
94. DE VEGA, vol. I, p. 212.
95. BEBBINGTON, J. 384, p.37.
96. MAYHEW, *London*, vol. I, p. 457.

Jack protected himself against robbers by putting a stone in a handkerchief in the shape of a sling. On one occasion when he was approached by two rough men, he quickly handed them a fancy watch, and they hurried away with it. He said he would have been happy to pay £10 to be rid of them, but the watch was only worth 8s [97].

Some pedlars carried a stout stick, but even this proved a disadvantage in the case of a travelling Jew known as 'Little Isaac'. He was found murdered in a wood near Plymstock, Devon. A militia man, Edward Jackson, said they met, and after drinking a pint of beer together left the inn. After a few miles Little Isaac felt tired and sat down for a rest, putting his stick behind him, whereupon Jackson picked it up and hit him several times, killing him. He then took Isaac's watch out of his pocket, and some goods out of his box, which he hid in a wood. On offering the goods for sale, and being asked how he came by them, he showed a Mr. Sherenbeare the box and "his conscience troubled him" so he confessed[98].

Another traveller, Jonas Levi, was killed by William Price, who dragged him into a wood, hit him with a stake, beating out his brains, so that several pieces of skull were later found in front of his body. Price robbed Levi of a guinea in gold and 2s 6d in silver and anything of value from his box. The Jews of Bristol promised a reward of £2 on conviction of the murderer. Having aroused suspicion by giving his sweetheart rings and trinkets, Price was arrested. He then had in his possession a new watch, strings of pearls and other valuable goods[99].

Wyatt of Fowey, invited the pedlar, Isaiah Fallo Valentine, to Falmouth to buy buttons or guineas. On making some excuse he took him to the quay, where he threw him into the water and suffocated him, and then robbed him of £260[100]. A ballad written "on reading the trial of the wretch of Dumfries 1821" recounts

97. HINDLEY, *Cheap*, p. 37.
98. *GM*, 1760, p. 43.
99. *GM*, 1754, p. 44; 1753, p. 588.
100. PICCIOTTO, vol. II, p. 286.

in *The Bloody Tragedy of Eskdale Muir* how a young pedlar boy was lured on to the moor and killed by a blow of an iron-shod clog, and all for a few trumpery combs, purses and such items[101].

Sometimes the robbery of pedlars' boxes was due to envious eyes on their contents. Moses Pincas, who had forty-four watches valued at £50, four bunches of pearls valued at £20, a silver snuffbox valued at 12s, a silver cup valued at 18s and 20 oz. of silver lace valued at £3 as well as a little cash, said of a thief "My box was open, he could then see my pearls and watches"[102]. After Newcastle Fair, Samuel Harris was robbed yet again of his box and all his money whilst he was asleep. He pursued the robber on advice from other Jews as to where the thief's relations lived, and after some months caught up with him and extracted £3 or £4 in return for a promise not to proceed against him[103].

Another typical merchant hawker, Henry Simons/Simmonds, came from the Continent to buy "Cloathes, watches and what I can get for money". He had 588 ducats with him which he carried in a leather purse "girded about my body". Some of the ducats had holes drilled in them as they had been part of his family's jewellery, and some were to be used to buy clothes and watches for the wife of Chancellor Corony, an important person in Henry's own country (probably Germany). With this in mind he tried to buy the Princess of Wales' cast-off clothing for £40 (he may well have been misled, or more likely misunderstood, as his English was almost non-existent). On his way to Bristol, where he wanted to visit the Synagogue, he spent the night at an inn. There he was attacked and robbed, his head was cut open and he was left penniless. He had to pawn his tallith (prayer shawl) as a result of his losses. The Overseer at the Great Synagogue in London, who used to see him "publikly and

101. *The Bloody Tragedy of Eskdale Muir*, Glasgow University Library, David Murray Collection NU I-XII.
102. OBSP, 1814, p. 81.
103. CLEGG, p. 47.

constantly" gave him a guinea from the poor box, and another time sixpence from his own pocket[104].

Later, after a series of encounters, mishaps and court cases, his erstwhile robber, Mr Ashley, indicted him for perjury, and he was only saved by the intervention of Mr. Franks, "the great rich Jew". The latter, with his lawyer, visited in haste all the members of the jury who had condemned Simons. They thereupon signed affidavits explaining they had misunderstood the Judges' directions. Simons won his final case, getting £200 for a mistake in the warrant apprehending him, and £470 on a promise not to bring an action against Ashley for malicious prosecution[105].

Isaac Solomon, too, was attacked and robbed in the afternoon between Rochdale and Manchester. Two men took:-

"Nine guineas
One Portuguese piece value £3.12s.
Three Moidores v. £4.15
Ten Shillings in silver and the goods hereafter mentioned being of the value of £10 and upwards viz.
Two pair of carved silver buckles
Two pair of silver tea tongs
One pinchbeck watch-chain
Four gold rings
One pinchbeck head for a cane
Ten pairs of crystal buttons
A silver watch-chain
Three silver stock buckles
One large silver clasp
A silver carved snuff-box
Several pairs of white metal buckles
Several Japan snuff-boxes and silver thimbles".

104. OBSP, 1755, p. 54.
105. The Case and Appeal of James Ashley, (Mocatta Library, B.A.37, SIM; BA37-ASH).

He advertised the loss but it is not known if he recovered anything[106]. The different types of money in his possession, of which he appears to have known the exact value, is noteworthy. He may well have been dealing with sailors, as in most ports the Jewish ships' chandlers or navy agents arranged the exchange of foreign coins for ships' crews returning from abroad. Moses Davis, who may have been a money-changer, stole fifty guineas from John Rowe (who was "up from the country") by pretending to accept John's claim to be paid twenty-eight shillings in notes for each guinea. There appears to have been well-known but illegal dealing of this type, the gold weight of the guineas was probably worth more than the legal twenty-one shillings[107].

Many Jews traded in sea-ports mostly in the South and West of England. In 1790, a letter from Government House Portsmouth referring to the propriety of enroling Jews in the Volunteer Corps, suggests it should be discouraged owing to "a great number of suspicious itinerant Jews at that time in town"[108].

The pedlars used to hire boats to go out to the ships or used boats of their own nick-named *Tailors Cutters*. On one occasion in Portsmouth harbour a tragic accident occurred. The pedlars had large quantities of goods with them and the over-loaded boat turned over when the sails gybed. The ships' boats saved ten men, two of whom died aboard. In all nineteen lives were lost[109].

Pedlars seem to have been in as much danger from attack on the Continent as they were in England. Samuel Harris en route for England, was robbed of all his money, by a waggoner[110]; and a pedlar in France who showed himself contemptuous of a Holy Well, was threatened with death. He, using his wits, quickly drank

106. *Gazette*, 10th March 1740, No. 7995, p. 5.
107. OBSP, 1812-1813, pp. 69, 74.
108. Wolf, BA 15.16.
109. *GM*, 1758, p. 91.
110. Clegg, p. 16.

some of the holy water, and declaring himself cured of rheumatism asked to be baptized. The peasantry freed him and before the appointed day for baptism he had disappeared[111].

Considering the hardships and dangers it is surprising to find one or two women peddling in the countryside; occasionally there are tantalizingly limited glimpses of these intrepid females. Sarah Ellis said she had been travelling for twenty-eight years, and always stayed in the best inns[112]; and Mary Jacobs used to travel with a basket selling peddlery ware, handkerchiefs and waistcoat pieces[113]. In 1741 Hannah Leppenwell took out a licence for travelling with a horse[114]; and in 1863 a pedlar on his way to Deptford said he travelled the country with a young woman who was tramping with him[115].

In spite of the dangers and hardships of a pedlar's life, there must have been some compelling attraction in it. John Bebbington left a good indoor job to take to the road again, with the excuse he needed some fresh air! Another old trader told Mayhew he had an old clothes shop, but tired of it and at last got rid of it: "Oh I walk both country and London still, I shall take a turn into Kent in a day or two"[116]. And Old Sammy travelled the roads although he didn't need to and indeed his rich brother gave him two guineas a week on the understanding he would stay at home[117].

Perhaps it was the freedom from the appalling slum life in the cities, the only alternative for these poor men, which led them to walk the roads and bear the cold, the danger and the loneliness that inevitably went with it.

111. *Jewish C.*, January 1881.
112. OBSP, 1738-41, p. 362.
113. OBSP, 1792-1793, p. 384.
114. PROK, A01 429/41.
115. Essex Public Record Office, EOA D/P 18/10. In the parish accounts for Essex, 1 shilling for a "travelling woman" appears.
116. MAYHEW, *London*, vol. II, p. 122.
117. HINDLEY, *Cheap*, p. 184.

CHAPTER II

PEDLARS' WARES

The goods the urban and country pedlars carried varied from completely practical, such as brushes, writing and sewing materials, to personal finery, cheap jewellery and watches, which were particularly prevalent, spectacles and so on[1]. There was a great gap between what the immigrant pedlars in their early days could afford: for example, pencils, combs, trinkets, and later, when some of them grew richer and sold quite expensive jewellery and silver. On the whole pedlars kept to a single type of goods, sometimes even fabricating them themselves. But some, like Alexander Abrahams, who was acquitted of receiving stolen goods, seems to have traded various articles at different times. Witnesses said that "he travelled the country with hardware", "he used to sell anchovies about", and "he used to sell pickles and anchovies"[2]. Likewise Abraham Cohen said he got a living by selling lemons and sometimes clothes[3].

In the nineteenth century old clo' hawkers of hats kept only to that article, the seller being also the maker, which accounted for their cheapness. Some pedlars did, however, add other goods to their stock. Isaac Hassan was carrying Jacob Hadida's box home for him, when he was attacked by two men who made off with the box. It contained as well as 12 oz. of rhubarb, 8 oz. of cloves, 6 oz. of mace, 9 oz. of cassia, 3.5 oz. cayenne, 1 oz. isinglass, 8 oz. of ginger and 8 oz. nutmeg,

1. See list in the Appendix.
2. OBSP, 1756, p. 167.
3. OBSP, 1781-1782, p. 85.

3 pieces of silk	value	£ 4		
3 crepe shawls	value	£ 2	2s	
9 crepe handkerchiefs	value	£ 1	7s	
24 thimbles	value	£ 1		
8 oz. weight of sealing wax	value	£	1s	
10 oz. of coral beads				
24 black lead pencils	value	£		9d
6 bottles	value	£		3d
5 oz. otto of roses	value	£	11s	
4 other bottles	value	£		6d
4 brooches	value	£	10s	
4 penknives	value	£	15s	6d
5 ounces silver	value	£ 1	2s	
17 other handkerchiefs	value	£ 3		

The box itself was found later lying empty except for some spices "the silks, coral beads and licence, all gone"[4]. A list of goods stolen from Henry Joseph's stall, when he left it to go in to warm his hands a little, is remarkably like those found in pedlars's packs, i.e.

8 pairs plated shoe buckles	value	2s
16 pair metal shoe buckles	value	3s
3 pair plated knee buckles	value	1s
3 pair plated stock buckles	value	2s
3 pair studs	value	2s
5 pair spectacles	value	3s
5 watch chains	value	2s
1 show glass (i.e. showcase)	value	2s.[5]

William Davenport, who let out lodgings to pedlars, explained to a law court where he was witness against Abraham

4. OBSP, 1824, p. 77.
5. OBSP, 1785-1786, p. 260.

Michelson, that among them "a good box" meant one which was well furnished with articles. He said that Abraham Michelson in conversation with Williams' wife, asked if Joseph Alexander, (who was a very hard working man and always paid his rent on the day it was due) had a good box, or a bad one. She replied it was a "midlingish" one. In fact it contained twenty sovereigns, a £5 note, fourteen gold rings, twenty-nine pairs of ear-rings value 9s, two scent boxes value 6s and twelve sovereigns, so it seems Alexanders' box contained articles in all worth a good deal of money, and yet did not qualify as a "good" one[6].

Occasionally pedlars did manage to move upwards in society, becoming costers, then shop owners and finally manufacturers or warehouse owners, supplying hawkers and shops. One such, Joseph Harris, began peddling needles, the smallest quantity being six for a penny. He gave the customers whatever size they wanted, and dressmakers and tailors bought packets of twenty-four for 2.½d. He later traded in watches, generally English ones, made to his special requirements, and he had his name marked on them. As his trade grew, he manufactured them himself[7].

It seems it was quite usual for watches, known in the trade as "Jew" watches, to be made specially for pedlars. In a trial at the Old Bailey a witness remarked, "I am very positive 'tis the watch for there was no mark or number on it, and I thought it had been made for the Jews upon that account"[8]. Another witness said "I showed him several (watches) then I took one down which was capped and jewelled in my name"[9], while Moses Lyon said "they are only the inside cases they all have my name and number upon them"[10]. According to Thomas Hawley of 76 The Strand, "the name engraved on the watch is the name that is known to the Public and which is over

6. OBSP, 1840-1841, p. 207.
7. HARRIS, p. 23.
8. OBSP, 1744, p. 47
9. OBSP, 1781-1782, p. 671.
10. OBSP, 1769-1770, p. 231.

the shop door[11]. Levy (1827), a pedlar, had watches manufactured by makers of all degrees, from the well-known master craftsman, Tomkin, to the cheap maker of watches, Levy of Liverpool, as well as very costly jewellery and cheap trinkets[12]. A retired watchmaker whom I met on a No. 55 bus, told me that up to 1920 "Jew" watches were still manufactured for pedlars. They were simple watches, fob type, and at that time were made of gun metal. The pedlar's name or his licence number was inscribed either on the inside or the outside of the back plate, just as formerly[13].

Quite a few pedlars made their own goods and if they could prove it, they were not required to carry a licence, which was a great advantage. Emmanuel Lemon made spectacles and sealing wax, the latter he sold to liquor merchants, presumably to seal their bottles[14]. This was in practice in 1837, when a vintner, recognizing some stolen ones, said "these bottles have my seal on them!"[15]

Joseph Solomon, who died in 1815, came to England at the age of thirty, having wandered about the Continent for fifteen years. He set himself up, on the death of the Duke of Cumberland, by buying black beads for necklaces. Later, after a disastrous spell dealing in old clothes, robbed of all his money, he returned to peddling, buying Bristol stone buttons and other small articles. Finally he learned to make "sundry small trifles in tin and wire" and was able to make his living and even save a little[16].

Jacob Kimhi, a well-known Turkish Jew of good family, sold slippers of all sizes and colours at one shilling and sixpence, or two and sixpence the pair. He was seen every day outside the Royal Exchange, or, during the hour of the Exchange in his "walk" in the Strand, Cheapside and Cornhill. When he was not selling slippers (and

11. OBSP, 1839, p. 271.
12. *Everyday*, vol. II, p. 533.
13. Personal information from a retired watchmaker.
14. *Repository*, vol. III, pp. 74-5.
15. OBSP, 1837-1838, vol. II, p. 278.
16. *Repository*, vol. III, pp. 74-5.

he never solicited buyers) he was busy writing learned Hebrew
commentaries and other religious works, for he was accepted as "a
sharp and well-versed scholar, a title which is generally reserved for
men of exceptional attainments", or quarrelling with the Synagogue's
lay committee about ritual affairs, in particular with the celebrated
quack Dr. Buzaglo. A well-known painter, Osias Humphrey, fascinated
with Kimhi's looks, painted his portrait. It is amusing to speculate on
how these two difficult and eccentric men got on with each other[17].

North African Jewish pedlars of whom there were at
least half a dozen in London at the end of the 19th century, generally
sold rhubarb and various spices, such as cummin, mace, cayenne and
white pepper, ginger and so on[18], though there is a portrait of one of
them, Aga Ismail, selling boot laces, and another, which may be of the
same man, selling lace, pins, etc[19].

Cheap Jack mentions a little wizened Israelite, with
seven or eight lbs. of rhubarb and a small pair of scales, with an ounce
and an ounce and a half weights. One rhubarb seller said he sold a
hundred ounces a week, weighing out small doses for children
according to their age. This man describes himself as "a Machan from
Durkey selling whulsul and retail"[20]. The rhubarb was called
"Turkey" or "Persian" according to its supposed provenance. Although
the rhubarb and spice sellers were all said to be North African Jews,
this is not entirely correct. In 1898 the police investigated two
Algerians, who are specifically called Mohammedans. They had used
other men's licences because they had been refused them owing to
their lack of English[21].

17.   JHSE, 1911-1914; Dushinsky, Kimhi & Buzaglo, p. 4; *Leisure* 1886,
p. 538; *Anglo*, p. 54, n. 999A; Rubens, pp. 42, 45; Anglo-Jewish Art and
Historical Exhibition 1956.
18.   Hindley, *Cheap*, p. 318.
19.   Rubens, p. 42.
20.   Hindley, *Cheap*, p. 318.
21.   PROK, MEPO 2/537.

The North African, Jewish pedlars were especially remarked owing to their picturesque clothing, unusual in the 19th century. This consisted of a long skirt or coat, baggy trousers, a wide cummerbund and a turban. An idealized pair of china figures (Red Anchor Chelsea 1754-8, or in some cases labelled Derby 1760), show a pedlar dressed in the fashion of the day in a flowered full-skirted coat and trousers, wearing a turban and carrying a tray full of bottles, his wife in a pretty contemporary dress. She has a box of trinkets in one hand and ribbons in the other[22]. Sometimes the man in this pair is different; he wears a striped instead of flowered trousers and a less full skirted coat, and carries a box of trinkets (quoted as Chelsea 1760)[23]. Yet another pair (1760-65 Bow) has the wife carrying the pedlar's box, plus a sack on her back and a small box with a keyhole on top of that. The man only carries a sack (old clothes?), has a purse hanging from his waist and a stick/pipe in one hand. He has a case on his hip and his mouth is wide open 'crying'. This pair, unlike the others, appear to be real portraits with shabby clothes and ugly faces. There is a faint suggestion of Chinese influence[24]. Some single male pedlars and old clothes men figures also exist, and these have more pronounced Jewish features, in some cases tending towards caricatures[25].

Morris Lissack (1851) mentions a man who regularly visited Bedford dressed as a bearded "Jerusalem Jew", in a blue coat, red cap with a large blue tassel and carrying a red umbrella — but who was not really foreign at all[26]. Other writers speak of a "Masquerading Turk selling genuine rhubarb"[27], and "a veteran Turk

22. Jewish Museum, London, Figure 693A; Luton Hoo Werner Collection.
23. *Victoria & Albert Museum Catalogue.*
24. Burrell Collection, Glasgow.
25. Jewish Museum, London.
26. LISSACK, p. 67.
27. HARVEY ALEPH (Pseud) *The Old City* (London, 1865), p. 225.

selling Rhubarb who has discarded his turban and now wears a Fez"[28].

In the same tradition a man known as "the Indian" wearing a white turban traded in the Scilly Isles from 1911 to 1950. He used to carry his goods in suitcases: pullovers, satins, silks, plush covers and tablecloths and sold them in the "off islands", i.e. the smaller islands near St. Mary's[29].

In a letter to the *Jewish Chronicle* in answer to letters in the *Morning Post*, a correspondent said that Irish itinerants pretended they were Jews, imitating their dress and manner of calling Old Clo'[30]; and some other pedlars dressed up as doctors or mechanics (i.e. workmen) to help them sell rather suspicious goods. The Reverend Brand saw "a regular ware room" in Westminster where those who earned their living by begging could hire widows' weeds, tattered rags, shabby genteel costumes, clerical suits, etc.[31].

Another type of pedlar, lemon and orange sellers, were generally young Jewish boys who hung about the stage coach yards and outside the inns where the coaches stopped to pick up passengers, pushing and urging the travellers to buy, they then dashed off to the next inn, where the following coach would stop, rushing for example from *Belle Sauvage* Ludgate Hill to the *Saracen's Head*, Snow Hill. The young boys later often became "apprenticed", though not in so many words, to old clothes men with whom they worked "half Rybeck" (possibly a Yiddish expression). In this case the older man put up the money and taught the boy about values in return for which the boys did the leg-work. They learned so fast they often started on their own after a few months. Oranges and lemons were also sold by

28. *The Freelance*, Manchester Scrap Book (Manchester), p. 125.
29. Mrs. Thomson & Mrs. Parry, St. Mary's, Isles of Scilly, personal communication.
30. *Jewish C.*, vol. III, Dec. 1849.
31. PLACE; *Birmingham Mercury*, Feb. 17th 1849.

4

women carrying them in two baskets, a flat one on their heads and a handled one on their arms[32].

The urban pedlars worked in towns with perhaps, forays into the country, and their "walks" were much shorter than the Old Clo' mens', as they did not have to search for their goods. With the coming of the railways the urban hawkers extended their range, walking into the country, and sending perishable goods on loaded carts, by rail, to meet them[33].

In town, the pedlars often stood in one position on part of their walk, like Kimhi at the Royal Exchange or Sole, who had been selling rhubarb for forty years and always stood outside Bow Church Cheapside, or Ben Aforiat who claimed St. Pauls' Churchyard[34]. In Manchester the gutter merchants were known among themselves as "the Kennel Pedlars" which indicates that they stood in the middle of the street where the Kennel ran, though the police were said to have taken very little notice of them[35].

There was also some door-to-door selling, chiefly by women pedlars carrying their goods in baskets. This was appropriately known as "going on the knocker". Fifty years ago (1937) most large town houses had a sign on the gate at the top of the steps leading down to the basement which said "no hawkers or circulars", to warn them off. Circulars were hawkers who had a settled round and called at regular intervals of approximately a month. In the remoter districts of the British Isles, they called, perhaps, once or twice a year, taking orders for any goods they were not carrying and delivering them on their next visit[36].

32. LAROON, *Cries of London*; RUBENS, p.42. For the expression Rybeck, see 66
33. ALEXANDER p. 78.
34. RUBENS, p. 42.
35. F. CORBIT, *Manchester Street Characters* (Manchester, 1870-1878), p. 2.
36. Mrs. Thomson, personal communication.

Both urban and country pedlars obtained their goods in "swag" shops, which supplied all their needs, but selling only in dozens. John Bebbington had to beg a swag shop dealer to allow him to buy ten tin cups and saucers because he only possessed 7s 5d[37]. They were sometimes able to buy from shop keepers who were willing to split their goods, or they could buy the shops' leftovers. The shop keepers were willing to sell at a cheaper rate to hawkers as they penetrated a market which would not in any case have been theirs, and some shopkeepers employed several hawkers to sell their goods. For this reason they were willing to give discounts on goods, or sometimes gave extra goods as a discount[38].

Because they had no capital when they first began to trade, the pedlars had to buy in small quantities. They also had to patronise warehouses for hawkers, called "slaughter" houses, which sold wholesale and retail, but were more expensive than the "swag" shops. Both "swag" and "slaughter" were supplied by makers of penny goods, most of which by the 19th century were imported more cheaply[39]. The swag shops bought on regular order, the slaughter houses on speculation.

The pedlars generally carried their goods in packs, which were square mahogany boxes with brass clasps. These hung round their necks by a leather strap, when open, and were carried hanging from the right shoulder when closed[40]. A gentleman of ninety-one living in the Scilly Isles, remembers a pedlar who, up to the second world war (c.1940) carried his goods in a typical 18th century wooden box with a strap over one shoulder. He also carried an ordinary suitcase containing his own clothes, which hung down his

37. BEBBINGTON, f. J 379.
38. ALEXANDER, p. 760ff.; Inverness, L/INV/BC 14/98A.
39. ALEXANDER, p. 77.
40. BUSBY.

back by a rope[41]. A lady from Shetland still possesses her father's box, which was made of leather[42].

Sometimes the pedlars carried their boxes slung over one shoulder held by a heavy scarf-like material, which finished tied round the waist. Busby describes a light strong box held before the body by a broad belt passing over one shoulder and under the opposite arm, and says the pedlars' large convenient pockets were also well filled[43]. Some boxes must have been made in a cheaper fashion as they are quoted on two occasions as being worth 2s; like the whitish deal box described by Aaron Mendoza[44]. When the lid of the box was open the small trinkets, buckles, scissors and so on could be seen fixed to it, the larger objects being within. Some had one to four drawers which could be pulled in and out, or perhaps lifted off like trays to show their separate contents; and one contemporary picture shows a box with little legs, so it could be stood on the ground.

Kirsh Landberg, a Polish pedlar, put his jewellery in a box valued at £1.4s.0d. and then in a bag costing 2s. When it was stolen it contained:

65 watches	value	£130.
7 breast pins	value	£ 10.
4 brooches	value	£ 5.
36 spoons	value	£ 9.
3 seals	value	£ 2.
6 rings	value	£ 20.
1.5 ozs of pearls	value	£ 25.[45]

---

41. Mr. Trenear (age 91), personal communication 1987.
42. Mrs. Hofman, personal information 1988.
43. Busby.
44. OBSP, 1769-1770, p. 98; 1777-1778, p. 422.
45. OBSP, 1847, p. 387; Inverness, L/INV/BC 14/98A. On one occasion a pedlar who had not enough room in his box had some of his goods in a friend's.

All the boxes were quite heavy. Levi Nathan complained his weighed (full) 41 lbs; and he was so tired humping it along the roads of France, he hired a horse though he couldn't afford it. Subsequently this intelligent animal walked home to its original stable, and Levi was obliged to continue without him![46]

Joseph Solomon, when he was robbed of all his money, hired himself out to carry another pedlar's box[47]; and after trudging the streets of London for eighty years, Levy also hired a lame Jew to carry his huge mahogany box for him[48]. When he was attacked by two men Isaac Hassan was carrying Jacob Hadidas's box on his shoulder, but this may have been because he was only going a short distance, and also, he had a saucer of pickles in his hand[49]. It was said Jewish pedlars refused to carry heavy articles, preferring showy Bohemian goods, which they could price as they saw fit.

Abraham Emmanuel describing the men whom he thought had stolen Israel Abraham's boxes whilst Israel spent the evening at *The Gentleman and Porter*, said that one thief was carrying a box on his head, while the other had a box under his arm. And one said to the other "d-m your eyes, why don't you bear a hand"? To which the man replied "I can't come faster it is so heavy". This is not surprising considering the contents, which Israel was in the habit of taking out: "I went out in the morning towards Hackney with my two boxes". The large one was worth 8s and the small one which was covered with shagreen (a type of snakeskin) 20s. They held:[50]

9 silver watches the outside cases covered with tortoishell	value	.50s
46 pair of silver shoe buckles	value	£20.00
4 pair silver knee buckles	value	.20s

46. NATHAN, *Short Account*, p. 33.
47. *Repository*, vol. III, pp. 74-5.
48. *Everyday*, vol. II, p. 533.
49. OBSP, 1824, p. 77.
50. OBSP, 1777, p. 422.

7 silver table spoons	value	£ 5.00
3 pair silver salts	value	£ 3.00
2 silver pepper castors	value	.40s
3 silver milk pots	value	£ 3.00
4 pair silver tea-tongs	value	.40s
5 silver punch ladles	value	.50s
40 gold rings set with stones	value	£20.00
12 cornelean seals set in silver	value	.12s
12 cornelean seals set in metal	value	.12s
7 pairs of silver shoe buckles set with stones	value	£7.00
12 silver pair pins	value	.12s

An almost life-size dummy board pedlar, in the Jewish Museum, gives a very good impression of the size and weight of the boxes[51]. But it must be remembered this figure can only be late, because it is made of plywood — though of course it could be a copy of an earlier one[52].

A porcelain figure of a pedlar (c. 1755/1760) in the V & A has what looks like a modern back pack, a flat board with a bundle strapped to it perhaps by leather thongs. There is an equivalent one in the Werner collection; bronze equivalents in the Wallace collection, and a picture in *The Everyday Book*[53]; so it may well have been a usual pattern.

Nothing if not ingenious, John Bebbington with only sixpence in his pocket, bought a herring box for a penny, covered it with blue paper, and hung it round his neck by strings. When he made some money, he remarked proudly that he now had "a proper Traveller's box with shoulder strap complete, quite a smart affair"[54]. "Old Sammy" had a "shallow", which was a flat basket about 3ft 5' by

51. On loan from Victoria and Albert Museum
52. Mr. Edgar Samuel, personal communication.
53. *Everyday*, vol. I, p. 1215.
54. BEBBINGTON, f. J. 379.

2 ft and 4 to 6 inches deep, weighing forty pounds. His stock consisted of spectacles, rhubarb, silver pencil cases, sponges, black lead pencils, earrings, wedding rings, pocket-knives, etc. He tied an oilskin cloth over it which he removed in a minute when he wanted to show his goods. His friends who had transport, would send or take his shallow ahead for him, and in return Sammy executed commissions for them and found cheap places for buying goods in London[55].

It is of interest that even the very late pedlars often continued to sell the same articles as the very earliest ones. For instance, Mr. Mellor, a well-known traveller in the Isles of Scilly (c.1920) sold pins, needles, sail needles, shoe laces, sewing cottons and silks and "bachelors' buttons". He was very proud of the buttons which could be fixed without sewing[56].

Occasionally pedlars, unlike the regular old clo' men, also sold old clothes from baskets. One of them, who was accused of giving false three shilling bits in change, used an oval basket. This was probably an unusual kind as a witness remarked upon it[57]. Baskets and trays could be hired for 1d a day. This type of itinerant was known as a "dragger", but the name also applied to thieves who stole from trunks on stage coaches and then brought actions against the coachman for the goods, and to others who cut off trunks from behind chaises and hackney coaches.

The 18th and 19th century pedlars of cheap jewellery in London, did not always carry boxes, some held up the gold charms and necklaces, for the customer to see, or had them hanging on their waistcoat, whilst the smaller pieces were kept in their pockets. They were often to be seen in public houses on market days, and most often at *The Jeweller's Arms* where they exchanged their trinkets with each other on a Sunday morning. Sometimes they bartered new jewellery for old, once in a way making a killing, by getting a really good piece

55. HINDLEY, *Cheap*, pp. 179-80; The Young Pedlar, Victoria and Albert Museum Print Room.
56. Mr. Trenear, personal communication.
57. OBSP, 1814, p. 152.

in exchange for a trumpery one. A certain amount of bartering odds and ends, old books, etc. for jewellery also went on[58], for instance a hawker called Lazarus bartered watches for old clothes[59].

The professional end of the trade had their centre at Thomas Tiddler's jewellery mart at the back of Phil's buildings in Houndsditch. Here, there was a large room, full of people, with long tables covered with gold and silver vessels, jewels, gold chains and bowls full of uncut stones[60].

Later (circa 1940) pedlars sold all kinds of tin kettles, tin pans, in fact tins of all kinds, which they carried "hanging about themselves". Around 1950 Indian pedlars carried suitcases, which was a suitable manner for their type of goods: satins, silks, plush table covers and cheap pullovers[61].

The early pedlars should not be considered in isolation. The streets of London in the 18th and 19th centuries were full of people selling different wares — lavender, cherries and strawberries in season, hot pies and chestnuts, sheets of music, brooms, etc. as well as others selling services, such as chimney sweeps, chair-menders and so on. The pedlars were only part of the throng, distinguished though, by their foreign looks and accents, and at least for some years, an alien type of life.

Apart from his box and his licence, the country pedlar's most useful possession must have been his almanac. Almanacs existed as early as 1685, but their make-up was slightly different from those

58. MAYHEW, *London*, vol. I, pp. 348, 261.
59. OBSP, 1819-1820, p. 192.
60. GREENWOOD, *Journeys*, p. 163. Seventy years ago, children played a game called "Tom Tidlers's Ground". The chant which went with it was "I'm on Tom Tidlers's ground picking up gold and silver".
61. Mr. Trenear, personal comment. Some of the earliest Jewish pedlars in America (1740) were tin pedlars or tinsmiths. The tin-plate was made from refined iron hammered and rolled into thin sheets and coated with pure tin. Many household goods were made from it (Connecticut Antiquarian 1951, No.2 "Tinsmiths and Pedlars").

which followed[62]. The early ones were, naturally, in English, and any pedlar using them would have been English. They contained lists of Fairs, arranged for each month of the year with the town and day on which they took place, the names of market towns and the day of the week on which the market was held, and a list of post roads and distances between towns.

In Laroon's *Cries of London* (1688) there is an engraving, entitled "Buy a New Almanac", of a pedlar woman with a basket on one arm full of almanacs, some open with playing card designs on the outside and some rolled up.

The earliest Jewish Pedlars' Almanac was published in Hebrew by J. Abendana in 1692, with further editions in 1693, 1694, 1695, 1696 and 1699. These were followed by N. Nieto's almanac in Hebrew and Spanish, dated 1717[63]. With the coming of the German and Polish pedlars, a series of pocket calendars were printed partly in Yiddish and partly in Hebrew, sometimes with a few English words written in Hebrew characters[64]. From 1782, Alexander produced almanacs continuously for forty years and by 1807 they appeared entirely in English except for some Hebrew dates. They contained the times when coaches arrived and set off, dates of Jewish Festivals, New Moon times and church holidays, as well as weather forecasts for most months, i.e. "this month is half dry and half wet", which may have been calculated on an average of a few years[65]. Each page also had biblical and historical details, such as, "Conversion of St. Paul", "Prince of Wales Birthday" and so on. There were also a great many advertisements for everything from Dr. Collis' cures to monumental masons and Jewish boarding houses. The early ones were smaller, and contained lists of cemeteries, Watchers, Jewish bath houses, the locations of Synagogues, names of Wardens, as-well as the usual

---

62. M.D. SPUFFORD, *The Great Re-clothing of England* (London, 1984), pp. 10-11.
63. JHSE, 12 (1931), p. 34.
64. ROTH, *Anglo*, p. 6.
65. M. MYERS. *Calendars of the Coaching Days*, JHSE, vol. 5, pp. 220-1.

holidays, and also lists of Jewish publications. One had a chronological table beginning with the birth of Abraham, followed by Daniel in the Lion's den![66]

The most useful information in these almanacs was probably that giving names of inns with dates and times of public coaches, such as "From London to Harwich", "Cross Keys", "Gracechurch Street on second and fourth Saturday mornings, five hours, the fare is .... shillings"[67]. An almanac of 1838-39 (Lindo's Jewish calendar) contains parcel rates, times of coaches from various pubs, newspapers and foreign letter rates, Watermen's fees, Hackney coach and Cabriolet fees, Law Terms, Holidays kept at Public Offices, Royal Birthdays, times of steam vessels from various docks, lists of Jewish charities, list of Synagogues and a calendar in English and Hebrew[68]. The calendar of 1838 is written entirely in English and contains the usual list of Festivals and Fasts as well as a list of charitable institutions and a short summary of Jewish history. All this extra reading may have come in useful for pedlars in passing lonely evenings in some pub on the road.

The Synagogue in general disapproved of calendars as they considered the dating of holy days inaccurate, but some were given their approval, as noted on the title page. One such was "carefully revised and correct by the Chief Rabbi"[69].

The son of the well-known publishers Alexander, who carried on his father's work of printing, publishing and translating the Jewish liturgy, found a dating error in a rival's publication and exploited it for all it was worth. One chief Rabbi, Moses Meldola, wrote "a new almanach for the year 5568 (1807-08) of the Christian era". It contained the New Moons, Full Moons, Quarters, Solstices, Equinoxes, Jewish Festivals and Fasts which are celebrated annually, together with the sections of the Pentateuch to be read every Sabbath

66. I. VALENTINE, *Almanac* (London 1838)
67. ROTH, *Anglo*, p. 6.
68. *Lindo's Jewish Calendar* (London, 1838).
69. M. MELDOLA, *A New Almanach*, (London, 1807-1808).

day, and also a table of the church and many other things curious and interesting. It also contained all the Royal Families' birthdays, beginning with George III (1733) to Princess Charlotte (1766) and for good measure a chronology of remarkable events such as the creation of the world, the Mishna, and the building of the new Portuguese Synagogue![70]

There is an apocryphal story of a Rabbi visiting a remote village where he was horrified to find the local Jews were keeping the Holy Days on the wrong dates. (Jewish festivals are moveable according to the Moon.) The local pedlar finally confessed he had regularly sold out of date almanacs to the inhabitants.

Cheap Jack said unsold almanacs were returned to the publishers after March, who then took off the leather covers and put the inside pages, which contained some good stories, into fancy coloured wrappers. These were then sold to the hawkers at 1s. 8d. the dozen, or £1 the gross, and they were disposed of at two for 6d[71]. As well as almanacs, booklets containing lists of fairs and their dates were published all over the country. These also contained the distances between towns, important for pedlars planning to arrive on the required day. The number of fairs is surprising. Fifteen towns' fairs are listed for Hertfordshire circa 1820, and there are forty one dates on which they took place. They appear, in general, to be tied to religious festivals, such as, the first Wednesday after Easter, the day after Holy Thursday, Palm Sunday, there was even one in mid-Lent![72]

Halsbury's *Laws of England* explains the difference between fairs and markets. Every fair is a market but not every market is a fair, the difference lying in the size and frequency of the gathering. Fairs are longer and occur once or twice a year, markets occur once or twice weekly. Some regular ones, such as Smithfield in

70. Ibid., pp. 22-3.

71. Albert Feather, personal communication. There is a list of almanacs in the *Anglo-Jewish Almanacs and Yearbooks* in the *Jewish Chronicle*, January 1936 supplement.

72. *Hertfordshire Almanach* (Hertford, 1814-1852) (Ephemerides).

London were for specific articles — cattle and sheep every Monday and Friday, and hay on Tuesday[73]. Important fairs such as St. Bartholomew's in London, had their own courts attached to them, to deal, on the day, with fines, tolls and disturbances. These were held at *The Hand and Shears*, a tavern near St. Bartholomews fair ground[74]. They were called "Pie powder" courts, perhaps from "pieds poudrés" the pedlars' dusty feet[75]. If so, the description admirably illustrates the long hard trek they had to take to be able to sell their wares.

73. *Owen's New List: Book of Fairs*, (London 1820) p. 46.

74. H.C. SHELLEY, *Inns and Taverns of London* (London, 1909), pp. 156-7.

75. R.W. MUNCEY, *Our Old English Fairs* (London, 1936), p. 159.

CHAPTER III

OLD CLOTHES MEN

The early Jewish settlers, who came to England in the 17th century during Cromwell's rule, were of Spanish or Portuguese origin. They settled in the East End of London in Duke's Place, Bishopsgate Street, Bevis Marks, St. Helen's Aldgate and the immediate area[1]. By 1792 the Jewish quarter was bounded by Bishopsgate in the west, Sun Street in the north, and by Aldgate and Houndsditch to the east and south respectively[2].

By the time the Dutch and German Jews arrived, c.1800, followed by the Russians and Poles, many of the richer Jews had moved out to semi-rural neighbourhoods. Their place was taken by poor immigrants and their families living in or near Houndsditch, Petticoat Lane (Middlesex St.) and Rosemary Lane (Royal Mint Street) in little houses in the slum districts of alleys and courts. With the influx of immigrants, the Jewish quarter expanded and by 1855 stretched north to High Street, Spitalfields, south to Middlesex Street and Houndsditch, east to Leadenhall Street, Aldgate and Whitechapel, while Bishopsgate remained the western boundary.

The Jews generally lived crowded together and by the 1890's there were further arrivals of immigrants which led to "whole blocks of buildings and streets being recognized as theirs" such as Cobb Yard, Wentworth St. and Roper's Buildings[3]. In Stepney Green beyond Whitechapel there were buildings which accommodated a hundred and seventy-eight families, of whom only twelve were Christian[4]. As a letter to the *Jewish Chronicle* remarked, "the foreigner feels more at home in the foreign quarter — the East End is the centre for foreign trades"[5].

1. RUMNEY, p. 1.
2. J. TIMBS, *Curiosities of London* (London, 1855), vol. I, p. 425.
3. BOOTH, *Conditions*, p. 45.
4. BOOTH, *Notebooks*, District 10, Non-Conformist Churches (183), p. 131.
5. *Jewish C.*, June 1899, p. 109.

The gradual take over of street after street by the Jews is illustrated in the notebooks of the social investigator, Charles Booth, where the mention of Jews moving into particular streets occurs with regularity. Some of his informants regarded this as an improvement, but on the whole it seems to have been resented, and those who were relatively better off moved out. Where the races were mixed in small courts, as yet unswamped by Jews, neither were pleased, and quarrels were frequent[6].

It seems that social prejudices kept the Christians and the Jews apart, Christians moving out of a street as the Jews moved in, though on at least one occasion the reverse was true. As late as the 20th century the races were still undeniably separate, the Jews living in Stepney (Whitechapel) the English in Wapping, while in St. Georges some streets were occupied by Jews, and some by Gentiles.[7]

Miss Macham, an early equivalent of a social worker, told Charles Booth that when the Jews fixed on a street they gradually pushed out the Gentiles, house by house, until they finished by evicting them completely[8]. They were, according to the Reverend Sakeld, able to do so, and incidentally raise the rents, as they were willing to pay sums of money to get the keys to a house. In spite of their propensity for overcrowding and some dirty habits, the Jews were, according to Miss Macham, scavengers who raised the whole tone of the district[9]. This is confirmed by a Select Committee witness who said that a terrible neighbourhood in which the people were steeped in crime and vice, became quiet when "these foreign Jews came and occupied the houses"[10]. Another clergyman in Bethnal Green who noticed the increase in Jewish occupancy, and (he thought) the consequent increase in English poverty, says it is bad for local tradesmen as the Jews dealt almost exclusively with their own people,

---

6. BOOTH, *Notebooks*, District 10, Non-Conformist Churches (183), p. 131.
7. W. GOLDMAN, *East End My Cradle* (London, 1940), p. 16.
8. BOOTH, *Notebooks*, XLVIII Clergy (228), p. 109.
9. BOOTH, *Notebooks*, Ibid., pp.109, 225.
10. BPP, *Select Committee on Immigration* 1889, p. 9.

although preferring an English doctor. This is borne out by a Jewish doctor (1746) who sneeringly complained of being unable to practise among his own people because they would not pay a living wage, though they gladly heaped gold upon a non-Jewish physician[11].

In spite of appalling conditions, the Jews were actually cleaner and lived more soberly than the English poor[12]. A French visitor to Whitechaple in 1842 said that their houses had more decent exteriors and the rooms were simple and clean[13]. Their vices, hotly denied by correspondents to the *Jewish Chronicle*, appear to have been gambling, which they delighted in, and a more than probable dabbling in petty crime. But most of the immigrants seized the life lines offered by the settled community of Sephardic Jews and later by their own people and took to hawking old clothes, or peddling[14].

In general the old clothes man was dressed in the same way as the lower classes, except for specific cases such as the Moroccan pedlars, but was very neat and clean[15]. A correspondent to the Editor of *The Times* in 1837 wrote that "the Jews though slovenly in their outward habit are remarkably cleanly in their persons"[16].

Around 1700 the old clo' men wore a long jerkin and cloak, with a hat (not, as often stated, a muff) in one hand, and in the other two or three swords to exchange for old clothes. They can be seen in many prints and engravings wearing a long, black or brown tunic, fastened by a girdle; later, in mid-19th century, this was followed by a loose frock-coat which resembled it[17]. Early hawkers are often pictured wearing a flat, wide-brimmed black hat, a three-cornered hat, or later still, a top hat.

11. BOOTH, *Notebooks*, District 10 (183), p. 45; Edgar Samuel, personal communication.

12. MAYHEW, *London*, vol. II, p. 120.

13. FAUCHER, p. 28.

14. *GM*, 1810, p. 557; see also above p. 8.

15. BOOTH, *Life*, vol. III, ch. IV, p. 35.

16. *Times*, 18/2/1832, p. 127.

17. HINDLEY, *Cries*, pp. 25-6.

In 1825 a description of an (actually fairly rich) old clothes man is as follows: "for the last eighty years has Levy trudged the streets of London and its environs ... bearing a beard of a dirty grey colour, some inches in length and divided in the centre, but coming from under and above the ears, over which was tied a gaudy red and yellow silk handkerchief, and a huge pair of heavy costly-looking silver spectacles. He wore a coat which had once been blue, the skirts whereof almost hung to the ground and were greatly in the fashion of a Greenwich pensioner; a velvet waistcoat with a double row of pearl buttons to which appended through one of the buttonholes, a blue spotted handkerchief reaching down to his knees; a pair of tight pantaloons which had evidently been intended for another, as they scarcely gained the calf of his leg, and from the fobs whereof were suspended two watch chains with a profusion of seals; and on his head was a hat projecting almost to points in the centre and back but narrow at the sides[18]. There is another description of a hawker, a regular visitor to a street "ill kempt, sallow, loud mouthed and yellow toothed" but extremely good natured in spite of teasing by naughty boys[19].

Old clothes men were distinguished by a bag, or sack, made of black Holland carried over one shoulder, or sometimes two bags to separate the better clothes from the rags, and up to four hats, one on top of the other, on their heads[20]. There is no explanation for this habit, which continued into the 20th century — it could have been to prevent crushing them in the bag. It was not purely a Jewish custom as it appears earlier on English hawkers, who also wore several hats, as can be seen in the engravings designed by Marcellus Laroon in the *Cries of London*[21]. There were five editions of the above prior to 1700, the earliest dated 1687.

18. *Everyday*, vol. II, p. 533.
19. BENNETT, p. 29.
20. HINDLEY, *Cries*, p. 26 (picture), p. 27; BENNETT, p. 39; JOSEPH, p. 10.
21. LAROON, *Cries*, "Old Coats, Suits or Coats" c.1688 (picture).

Although contemporary artists from the 17th century onwards represented them in this way, Charles Hindley wrote that he had never seen a hawker with more than one hat on his head[22], while the many porcelain figures, though sometimes holding two hats, never have more than one hat on their heads[23]. In 1887 Tuer wrote that the old clo' men are nearly always represented as in the Catnach illustrations wearing several hats, but that though "he may often be met with more than one in his possession he is now seldom seen with more than one on his head." Against this, however, is the following rhyme in Sam Syntax's *Cries* (1884):

> Four hats on his head
> Boots slung o'er his arm, a bag on his shoulder
> Mo stops at the door, while a coat Susan shows,
> 'A ferry good bargain, Old Cloash, Old Cloash'.[24]

As each load of immigrants became anglicized in their dress, a fresh tide would arrive wearing their characteristic ethnic clothes. One description speaks of Polish Jewish pedlars in high boots and fur hats[25], and in 1780 no one in the Jewish congregation of Falmouth was allowed to be called to the Law (an honour vaguely equivalent to reading the Lesson in a Christian church) if he was wearing Jack boots outside his trousers, a coloured handkerchief round his neck, or chewing tobacco![26]

Most of the hawkers wore beards which was not usual at that time (c.1793) as is clear from a line in *Aaron's Show Box*, a satirical poem, "You will not be of Jews so shy when beards come into fashion."[27] That it was taken as natural for Jews to have beards is

22. HINDLEY, *Cries*, p. 27.
23. TUER, p. 61.
24. S. SYNTAX, *Cries of London*, c.1824, Guildhall Library (PAM. 3645).
25. BOOTH, *Notebooks*, 13 FB (351), p. 67.
26. WOLF, B29, London 1780.
27. Mocatta, Pamphlets (Box).

5

shown by Cheap Jack, a pedlar who wrote "and Harry Jessel being a Jew, wore a very long black beard"[28]. Not all Jews were bearded, though, as Wendeborn noted that German Jews wore beards, Sephardic, Spanish and Portuguese did not[29]. Tuer mentions a bearded, side-curled moustachoied Jew, in a long coat, wide brimmed hat and Wellington boots[30]; and a note in the Plymouth Congregation's minute book (1779) records the excommunication of a member for cutting his beard during the first nine days of August (a religious period of mourning)[31]. According to Southey no particular dress was required of them by law, but the lowest types let their beards grow and wore a sort of black tunic and girdle[32].

A witness in a court case remarked that a particular man was "dressed as a costermonger", but said he did not know if he was one because it was a very common dress for men who sold nuts and oranges; so he may well have been referring to a pedlar's type of dress[33].

Early 20th century idiosyncratic old clo' men wore a scarf round their necks, knotted twice and tucked into a collarless shirt, with a waistcoat, old trousers, held up by braces, a flat cap known as a "fish slice"[34] and Wellington boots "as they had to walk into all kinds of muck"[35].

The old clothes men rose early, soon after sunrise in summer, and while it was still dark, in winter, and worked till fairly late. They started out with a guinea or two in their pockets with which to make the day's purchases[36]. These poor men had arrived penniless

28. HINDLEY, *Cheap*, p. 110.
29. WENDEBORN, vol. II, p. 470.
30. TUER, p. 61.
31. WOLF, on a small piece of paper in "Provincial Jewries".
32. SOUTHEY, p. 396.
33. OBSP, 1862-1863, vol. II, p. 485.
34. Taxi No. 7.
35. Taxi No. 3.
36. ATKINS, p. 60; *GM*, p. 557.

in England, and, as in the case of the pedlars, it was their richer co-religionists who lent or gave them a minimum amount (two pounds) to enable them to begin trading. Sometimes this was repaid on a weekly or monthly basis[37]. Occasionally they might borrow a pound from a neighbour, or a pub owner, money which had always to be repaid, as any further loans depended on this. In the case of pub owners the interest payable was 2d a day for 2s, 3d a day for 5s; 6d for 10s and 1s for a pound[38].

After the hawkers left home in the morning, many would go to one of the coffee houses near where they lived, such as those in Houndsditch. Here, they would have breakfast, which seems to have been all they would eat until they arrived home in the evening[39]. *Sam's* coffee house was one which catered for Jews and provided an accommodation address for business men[40]. Owing to a (late?) correction in the legal document of 1779 selling the lease of this coffee house, it is unclear whether the name *Sam's* was used before the name *The King's Head and Rose* or vice versa, as Mayhew appears to think. *Benjamin's* coffee house was another known meeting place for the Old Clothes Men[41], as was *The Jeweller's Arms* where they met on Sunday mornings. *The Ship and Star* in Rosemary Lane was also a public house frequented by persons dealing in clothes, and other things[42], and a coffee house called *Tom's* near Dukes Place sold wine and brandy and had as customers all the Jews of the neighbourhood, except another coffee house keeper![43]

Bachelors ate in eating houses kept by Jews, and though it was said that some might nip into a Christian eating-shop if no one was looking, it seems very unlikely. These men were so imbued with

37. GEORGE, p. 128 ff.
38. ALEXANDER, p. 71.
39. MAYHEW, *London*, vol. II, p. 120.
40. ROTH, *Synagogue*, p. 66.
41. MAYHEW, *London*, vol. I, p. 87.
42. OBSP, 1824-1825, p. 218.
43. OBSP, 1784, p. 12.

their religion they are known to have suffered hunger rather than break its laws[44]. During the day they might eat some dry bread and drink water, and though accused of begrudging themselves a bite to eat for fear of losing a deal, it was more likely they were obeying religious dictates which did not allow them to eat non-Kosher food under any circumstances[45]. Moses Jacobs who "would live on the smell of an oil rag" liked to work all day and all night too... He didn't eat all day except for "a tuppeny buster, a small bit of butter and some wishy-washy coffee[46]. Zangwill describes a traveller, Moses, as living chiefly on dry bread and black tea, out of his own cup — with meat and fish completely banned by religious law, even when he could afford them [47]. Levi Nathan, an old clothes man too, was afraid to touch non-Jewish food and was almost starving (he implies) because the Jews would not sell or give him any food at all, owing to their disgust at the way he treated his wife. He drank tea all day long and was always thankful to anyone who would allow him to boil up some water for it[48]. In the evenings, some hawkers liked to go to pubs, where they would eat. Hyman Moses said he went to *The Blue Anchor* every night for fourteen or fifteen years[49].

Every old clo' man had his "walk" and they never impinged on each other's. If they had to pass through another man's territory, they stopped calling their wares. Sometimes they agreed to share a walk, in which case each would take a different street, and share their profits at the end of the day. This was known as "half Rybeck" or "Kybeck", and was also resorted to when the young boys were learning the trade, though the business more often than not was

44. BOOTH, *Life*, vol. III, p. 35.
45. MAYHEW, *London*, vol. II, p. 119.
46. HINDLEY, *Cheap*, p. 191.
47. ZANGWILL, p. 55.
48. NATHAN, p. 36.
49. OBSP, 1801-1802, p. 158.

passed from father to son[50]. Jewish children began to work very early, sometimes at eight or nine years old[51].

The walks could be quite long, and even in town a man might travel fifteen miles in a day wet or shine, as a little contemporary rhyme has it:

> He has travelled many miles today,
> And many he must travel yet
> Though his heart is heavy
> And his garments wet[52].

As they walked along, hungry and tired, a full bag hung over one shoulder, they would be on the look out for customers, peering down into basements or up at windows and into shops:

> When old clothes I'm crying
> Down areas I'm prying
> To catch vat suits buying
> For full dress night tramps![53]

A verse below an etching in one of the *London Cries* series, draws a picture of the old clothes man:

> The Jew would down the area peep
> To look for custom underground
> His bag he o'er his shoulder flung

---

50. BOOTH, *Life*, vol. III, p. 35. "Rybeck" may be derived from "revar" which means "profit" in Hebrew. I should like to thank Rabbi Friedlander for this information.

51. SOAS. Archives of the Council for World Mission. Mission to the Jews in London, Frey's letters.

52. WRIGHT, p. 276.

53. Universal Songster (London, 1825); *Zedekiah the Jew*, p. 379.

And to the footman sweetly sung
"Cloash to sell" etc.[54].

The walks included the lowest, to the highest class neighbourhoods, the poorer quarters having more goods for sale, but of a lesser quality than those in richer areas[55]. Their first, very early calls would be on the men of Billingsgate, Newgate, Smithfield and Leadenhall markets[56]. Some said the men bought from the rich, or the servants of the rich, to sell to the poor[57], but this is not strictly the case, as, for instance, they liked districts frequented by sailors[58]. The Jewish old clothes men never walked the streets at night, they would go the marine stores in the mornings to buy clothes which had been left the previous evening:

When boys and girls are sleeping sound
Old Levi takes his early round.
From street to street he wanders wide
Will stand with clothes on either side,
Now maids produce your tattered store,
And sell them quickly at the door[59].

In the more aristocratic parts of London, in the West End, they found much of their trade in the mews at the back of the houses. Here, lived the coachmen and their families above the stables, and also some of the men servants who might have their master's cast-offs for sale. These too, were among their early calls, as the coachmen and grooms were up, grooming the horses and cleaning the

54. RUBENS, p. 45.
55. *Leisure*, July 1956, p. 491.
56. PYNE, p. 242.
57. ENDELMAN, p. 181 ff.
58. BOOTH, *Life*, vol. III, p. 36.
59. New York, 42 Street Library, *The Cries of London* (c.1790).

carriages[60]. The Old clothes men also bought old livery, harness, linen, cloth, coach glasses (i.e. windows), saddles, in fact every article even seemingly worthless ones[61]. A hawker said he dealt with Hackney men (Hackneys were a type of hired coach) for hammer cloths and harness, as well as dealing in old clothes[62].

They frequently walked the mews behind Barracks, because the gold torn from uniforms was greatly prized[63], as the following rhyme which appears beneath a *Cries of London* 1823, shows:

> Old clothes you often hear him say
> Perhaps you've some to sell today
> And you should see his smiling face
> At sound of gold or silver lace.

Another of their regular visits was to the hulks in the Thames where prisoners were kept before their transportation. They would have an arrangement with the captains, and even if they offered only half-a-crown for a suit the prisoners were obliged to accept, as they were not allowed to keep their own clothes[64]. At Woolwich, old clothes man Myers bought clothes from the Naval officers. He was very careful about buying articles from people bringing things that did not belong to them. Speaking of one client, he said firmly, "If he had bought a watch or gold lace, I should have said 'sailors do not belong to gold lace'"[65].

The old clothes men preferred to deal in the small streets where middle class families lived. This was where barter would come into play as the ladies liked china ornaments and glassware, and

60. PYNE, p. 242.
61. OBSP, 1776-1777, p. 302.
62. OBSP, 1781-1782, p. 272.
63. ZANGWILL, p. 2.
64. R. HUGHES, *The Fatal Shore* (London, 1987), p. 139.
65. OBSP, 1844-1845, p. 176.

were happy to exchange their own and their husband's old clothes for these articles. One man got "a new great coat in exchange for a few trumpery tea things"[66], and another obtained a whole suit in exchange for two geraniums[67].

The ladies from the better houses were ashamed to be seen talking to an "Old Clo'" man and would hustle him indoors, but they were expert at bargaining and would want a whole dressing table service for a few worn out waistcoats.

> Clo, Clo, have you any old clo?
> I've glasses and china a splendid show
> Trousers and coats, no matter how old
> I'll change for china covered with gold[68].

It must be said the hawkers' china and glass on offer was of an inferior kind, the glass even "won't stand hot water"[69]. There is mention of women with baskets of damaged crockery to be bartered for old clothes from door to door[70]; and of a young Jewish woman carrying a small basket full of all kinds of glass and crying "Clo". But this was extremely rare, as Jewish women hardly ever undertook this kind of work[71]. Although almost exclusively a male occupation, there were at least one or two women old clothes hawkers such as Sarah Israel who "only lived in a single room" and "went about the streets crying old clothes"[72], and Jayne Payne who also dealt in them[73]. There is an unusual picture of an old clothes woman

66. BOOTH, *Life*, vol. III, p. 29.
67. *ELM*, May 1891, p. 294.
68. HINDLEY, *Cries*, p. 154.
69. BOOTH, *Life*, vol. III, p. 29.
70. GREENWOOD, *Journeys*, p. 57.
71. BOOTH, *Life*, vol. II, p. 125.
72. OBSP, 1781-1782, p. 27.
73. OBSP, 1790-1791, p. 194.

dated c.1780, but she has no sack or outward sign of her trade, except for a large basket[74].

In general Jewish hawkers disliked trading crockery for clothes, as it was heavy to carry, weighing sometimes as much as three quarters of a hundredweight. This part of the trade therefore fell into the hands of strong young Irishmen[75]. As an old Clo' man complained, no sooner had he got rid of some crockery than he replaced it with the weight of old clothes[76]. This trade continued until the twentieth century. In Scotland as late as 1977, the *pig wife* came round with a horse and cart full of china and stone hot water bottles known as *pigs*. She exchanged the china for rabbit skins, feathers and rags[77].

As well as buying from houses, the men often bought or sold by chance in the streets. A girl said she saw Philip Abrahams buy a dress from an old clo' man in the street before she could make an offer for it. Asked if she often bought things in this manner, she replied "Yes we frequently do"[78]. Pasco Aronson, who was a traveller, asked an old clo' man coming along Shoreditch if he had got anything "in my way", as he often dealt with him[79]; and John Dick was crossing Petticoat Lane when Mordecai the Jew stopped him, and offered him some glass he wanted to dispose of[80]. As for David Mendes, he bought a bundle of handkerchiefs while he was sitting in a coffee house; and Samuel Smith, who said when he had money he bought anything he could, bought dresses (at least on one occasion) in the street, and sold them there too[81].

74. Picture in Guildhall Library London, 21.21.

75. MAYHEW, *London*, vol. II, p. 1101.

76. BOOTH, *Life*, vol. III, p. 30.

77. Edinburgh, Scottish Material Culture Archive, MS. Lady Maitland (1977).

78. OBSP, 1751-1755, p. 95.

79. OBSP, 1791-1792, p. 60.

80. OBSP, 1830-1831, p. 199.

81. OBSP, 1809-1810, p. 298.

As the Old Clo man went on his way, searching for wares, and doing his best to attract the attention of likely sellers, he used, as did street vendors of all types, to "Cry".

The kind of cry for old clothes varies a little in contemporary descriptions. In general they relied upon the snapped off short words "Clo" or "Old Clo", or "Old Clo', old clo' clo'"[82]; or sometimes "Clo' sale, clo' sale, clo'"[83].

Longer cries were "Cloashes to sell, cloashes round and sound"[84]; "old rags, old jags, old bonnets, old bags", or "Cloashes to sell, any old bottles, or phials to sell or broken glass"[85]. Pieces of broken glass were sometimes bought for making chandelier drops[86]. It seems to have been a regular trade as Henry Samuel for example went about buying vials and broken glass[87].

The cries changed over the years. In the early edition of Laroon's *Cryes of London* the old clo' man's cry is "Old doublets", while in the slightly later one it is "old suits, old cloaks, old coats"[88]. In the Jewish districts they would cry "old Rek" which is Yiddish for "old coats"[89], and an early 20th century cry was "old rags, old bones", accompanied by a clanging bell; and another was "old rags, old lumber"[90].

A modern book of old street cries speaks of a man with a wonderfully rich and powerful voice and a multiplicity of trades at his command, and gives the musical notation of his cry, with the words "any rags, or bones, boots or shoes, any umbrellas to mend"![91]

82. RUBENS, p. 48.
83. *Universal Songster* (London, 1825), p. 22.
84. RUBENS, p. 45.
85. RUMNEY, p. 229.
86. OBSP, 1817, p. 174.
87. OBSP, 1809, p. 491.
88. TUER, p. 61.
89. Mrs. Debina, personal communication.
90. Taxi No. 4.
91. KING, JEWELS & CHILD, *Old Tyneside Street Cries* (Newcastle, 1924), Newcastle Chronicle, pp. 56-7.

In 1987 a London taxi-cab driver obliged me by getting out of his cab and tunefully singing "old rags, old bones, any old metal", which had been his trade for many years[92].

Perhaps because of their foreign accent the men were said to cry with "a peculiarly harsh and guttural sound"[93], "the most nasal and extraordinary sound", "a plaintive yell"[94], "a monotonous cry"[95], "a shout"[96], "a bleat"[97], or even, by an elderly hawker, "a meek twitter"[98]. Of course the cries would have had to be piercing to be heard above the street noises, and in particular to drown many other street cries[99].

One man carried a Dutch clock which he rang continually, to reinforce his cry[100]. As lat as 1897 there were complaints about street cries on Sunday. Henry Lazarus who lived in Tavistock Square wrote irate letters to the Commissioner of Police about "shouting and yelling hawkers" and even threatened to take the Vestry to court, which he had already done on two occasions, to induce them to look after the poor peoples' houses and not neglect them[101]. Legal advice to the Police was, in this case, to use remonstrance and to avoid the strict enforcement of the law which would involve the seizure of the hawkers' goods. As for the cries, the advice continues, the voice is not considered a noisy instrument!

92. Taxi No. 4.
93. SILLIMAN, p. 270.
94. CHESNEY, p. 191.
95. RUBENS, p. 42.
96. ENDELMAN, p. 182.
97. MAYHEW, *London*, vol. II, p. 119.
98. ZANGWILL, p. 2.
99. DAVIS, p. 49.
100. BENNETT, p. 39.
101. PROK, MEPO 2/368. The ecclesiastical parish or vestry was a unit of local government. By the 18th century in London, its duties included the upkeep of the church and the relief of the poor. The information derives from numerous County Archive Minute Books.

Curiously, Henry Lazarus' letter is headed by a coat of arms with Hebrew writing incorporated in it[102].

The police, or earlier the watch, seemed to be rather wary of interfering with hawkers. In 1739 a remark in *The Gentleman's Magazine* warned "Let it not be forgotten in the case of Hawkers and Pedlars a certain minister was obliged to take shame to himself"[103].

Coleridge irritated by a hawker's raucous cries asked an old clothes man why he couldn't say plainly "old clothes". The man looked at him gravely, and replied with an excellent accent, "Sir, I can say "old clothes" as well as you can, but if you had to do so ten times a minute for an hour together you would say "ogh Clo" as I do now". Coleridge owns he was so taken aback that he ran after the man and gave him a shilling, which was all he had with him[104].

Hawkers in the North did not cry their wares, though old Tyneside street cries are known, but in London the cry of "Clo, clo" was heard all over the town from the most aristocratic to the poorest quarters[105]. The old clothes man, later known as "rag and bone" men, continued to "cry" well into the 20th century, long after other street cries were no longer to be heard.

As time went on most of the old clothes men no longer walked the streets, except for a few elderly ones, and were gradually replaced by cockneys, or rough heavy-drinking Irish. Many of the Jewish hawkers had become owners of warehouses which might consist of a simple shop with a yard behind it, or a quite large building. Those who were still hawking continued to carry bags and they dealt only in second-hand clothing; the others had barrows or carts drawn by donkeys and collected mainly rags[106]. The donkeys and horses were stalled in London, one stable was in Hackney, another

---

102. PROK, MEPO 2/368.
103. *GM*, 1739, p. 318.
104. COLERIDGE, p. 104.
105. FELIX, p. 11.
106. Mrs. Debina, personal communication.

in North Kensington[107]. The horses could be trusted to find their way home on their own, which was useful if they were taking their masters home from the pub![108]

As there were a good many warehouses competition for goods was fierce, and the hawkers could argue about the prices offered[109]. Right into the twentieth century barrow men in Islington had very large scales on their barrows and people brought bundles of rags to be weighed and paid for there and then. These barrow men had hand bells which they rang to attract custom[110].

In the warehouses, after the rags were sorted from wearable clothes, they were further sorted into cotton, worsted or knitted wool. Rows of sacks were fixed by ropes and pulleys to the ceiling, and the various types placed in them and hauled up out of the way till needed. Some of the better clothes, as in earlier times, were given to women 'out' workers to mend and turn, and were then sold to second-hand shops. Women were also employed to strip the lining from coats before they were sorted. Coats were usually baled and sent to the quays to be forwarded to third world countries. Ends of cloth, known as "Fents" and ragged clothes were sent to Austin's Wharf, and thence to northern factories, to be made into "shoddy"[111]. In the late 19th and early 20th centuries this was a poor type of cloth, used for making *slop* suits, a down-market suit made up by women — but later it became much improved and was used for uniforms, carpets, covers and so on.

The gradual change from retail to wholesale which runs beside the continuation of the hawking and peddling was more

---

107. Taxi No. 3.
108. Taxi No. 10.
109. Mrs. Debina, personal communication; OBSP, 1849, p. 255. In 1849 the price of rags for five bags weighing 8 or 9 hundredweight, was £5; by 1857 the price had fallen to 1d per lb, or 5s the hundredweight, and in 1950 rags were bought by the hawkers at 3d the lb.
110. Taxi No. 1.
111. Mrs. Debina, personal communication.

apparent than real. Certainly the hawkers and pedlars died out, but the street-trading in clothes continues till today in the second-hand stalls of our cities and towns.

CHAPTER IV

CLOTHES EXCHANGES AND RETAIL SALES

The old clothes dealing district where the hawkers used to bring their goods, was first mentioned by Stow in 1598[1]. An early description says, "the hawkers of old clothes carry their goods to Rag Fair, a place in the middle of the street near the Tower"[2]. This headquarters was a space about ten yards square adjoining Cutler Street, White Street, Carter Street, and Harrow Alley. The indescribable noise and confusion which went on attracted complaints from the local inhabitants. In 1701 several inhabitants from the "Upper Hamlet of Rosemary Lane in the Parish of Whitechapel" presented a petition to the Justices of the Peace complaining that "dayley meetings are held and kept in the hamlet on pretence of a custom of keeping a fair .... which is called Ragg Fair. ... The meetings are a very great hindrance and disturbance .... and those meetings are to buy and sell stolen goods and for the encouragement of all manner of wickedness"[3]. The petitioners asked for the fair to be suppressed and perhaps as a result a court order was issued stating that "an unlawful and riotous meeting is dayly held in this public highway and streets in and about a street called Rosemary Lane .... for buying and selling old goods wearing apparel and other things (greatly supposed to be stolen) .... and to the common annoyance of the inhabitants of the neighbourhood and the other of his Majesties' subjects passing by and through the way and streets ... and such meetings and assemblies must be suppressed"[4]. This is, as far as can be seen on the rather worn paper, by order of the Court to the High Constable of the Tower.

At a later date (1743) there was a petition from the inhabitants in and around Monmouth Street which also complained of obstructions and hindrances "owing to the many people who come

---

1. JOSEPH, p. 9.
2. ATKINS, p. 60.
3. *GLRO*, MJ/SP, 1701, Jan. 1st.
4. *GLRO*, MJ/SP, 1701, Jan. 2nd.

everyday to buy and sell old rags and other old things" and "they say it is a common nuisance to all the inhabitants as well as the Almswomen". In a final attempt to persuade the Justices of the Peace to order their removal the petition pointed out that "several of the said rag sellers by reason of their poverty are likely to be chargeable to the said Parish" — no doubt a very telling argument[5]. A later but almost identical complaint appears in Glasgow (1839) signed by a number of inhabitants of 63 Bridgegate against the old clothes dealers who "choked up the entry to their houses"[6].

In 1782 the Vestry of the Minories was continually troubled by "the Jews and other people in front of the Minories", and incurred some expenses in driving them away. In 1788 there are again complaints of "the stoppages occasioned by the Old Clothes People", and the Church Committee decided that they were a nuisance and ought to be removed. Consultations with the magistrates and the delivery of one thousand hand bills (probably warning of dire consequences) by the Beadle to the hawkers had no effect, for in 1789 the Vestry sent a Committee to consult Mr. Justice Staple on the most effective way of preventing "the nuisances in the Front occasioned by the old clothes hawkers", and they decided to deal with them according to law. No more is heard till 1896 when a certain Mr. Sly had to be dealt with for a similar offence[7].

A forerunner to later exchanges, circa 1776 was a kind of meeting place in *The Duke's Head*, Saint Marten's Street, Leicester Fields, where the old clothes men bought and sold to each other[8]. It may have been the club where old clothes people met of which Levi Nathan speaks[9]. It would have been used solely for dealing and not for the general public.

5. *GLRO*, AM/PW/1743, 61; MS/SP/TEMP ANNE/1.
6. Glasgow, Mitchell Library, E/1/1/19.
7. E.H. TOMLINSON, *A History of the Minories* (London, 1907), pp. 333-4.
8. CBSP, Dec. 1776 - Oct. 1777 p. 199.
9. NATHAN, p. 1.

By 1805 the trade which had been carried on in the open in Rosemary Lane (Royal Mint Street) and Petticoat Lane was soon to find a new home when two enterprising firms opened Old Clothes Exchanges. A Mr. Lewis Isaacs bought the houses which enclosed the back of Philip's Building, thus making room for an exchange which measured 100 ft by 70 ft.[10]. This was reached by two narrow lanes, and had an entrance in Houndsditch[11]. It was a large plot of damp ground through which one or two thousand passed daily, surrounded by a hoarding with a narrow projecting roof just wide enough to shelter one person. In the middle there were four rows of chairs back to back[12]. It became "a receptacle for every article which is collected in London and its environs and for fifteen to twenty miles around and they are brought there day by day and sold to parties who are called 'forestallers'". These were the middlemen who bought the goods to sell again, either wholesale or retail. Two hundred years earlier 'forestallers' bought goods for resale at great profit and as this was considered illegal they had been banned from the town[13].

The date the Exchange was opened is often quoted as 1843, but a series of engravings by Craig of various pedlars in well-known streets and squares dated 1805, in a book entitled *Modern London* proves it to be earlier. A description facing a picture of a pedlar in Fitzroy Square says that there was a commodious old clothes exchange adjoining Rosemary Lane which unfortunately, in spite of all attempts to persuade them, the old clothes men constantly abandoned in favour of their old haunts in the streets "to the annoyance of all who pass that way between twelve and three"[14].

10. MAYHEW, *London*, vol. II, p. 26.
11. FAUCHER, p. 33.
12. MAYHEW, *London*, vol. II, p. 39.
13. J. STOW, *The Survey of the Cities of London and Westminster*, ed. J. STRYPE, 2 vols. (London, 1754-5), vol. II, p. 413.
14. Sir R. PHILLIPS, *Modern London* [Fitzroy Square, picture] (London, 1805), picture & facing page.

6

As time went on however, they grew accustomed to the new order, and from half past two till five o'clock or possibly, according to another commentator, till eight o'clock in summer, and until between two and four in winter, it was to the Exchange, amidst the mounds of rags and tatters, that the hawkers brought their sacks bulging with the day's purchases. They would seize a chair and empty their sack on the ground, the buyers pouncing on the clothes, picking them over and haggling over the price[15]. Some of the old clothes men carried the articles they had for sale on outstretched arms, but most of them carried their wares in bags. It cost a halfpenny entrance fee, except on Saturdays and Sundays, when it was free, as there was little business, and anyway there was no trading on Saturday until after sundown[16]. The usual toll rose to 3d for country hawkers.

The trade in old clothes had its slack times, that is, right through the winter till spring, the best season being in early spring and right through the summer.

By 1845 there were three exchanges, all near Petticoat Lane, but only two are described in contemporary literature[17]. Isaac's Exchange was a place "where swarm and chatter among themselves the real old clo' men and women". "We passed through a great crowd of dirty ragged people to the number of some hundred, they appear to be very busy displaying and examining the old clothes which they were pulling out of bags" remarks a visitor to the site. "Exposed for sale are silk gowns and satin gowns, costly laces and shawls of Persia and India, tarnished certainly, but still with a thoroughbred air about them[18].

By 1849 the place had changed a little. Now there were rows of benches, covered by narrow pitched roofs supported on beams

15. MAYHEW, *London*, vol. II, p. 39.
16. MAYHEW, *London*, p. 28.
17. OBSP, 1844-1845, p. 416.
18. SILLIMAN, p. 270.

but open at the side to wind and rain, which was said to be a good thing as the air blew away the musty smells[19].

Cheap food and drink vendors added to the crowds amidst an appalling smell that reached everyone's nostrils from streets away. According to a letter to *The Times*, "even after night has fallen and the crowds withdrawn the stench in the streets is beyond endurance"[20].

Contrary to the impression generally given, the old clothes trade was not primarily one of buying and then refurbishing hawkers' goods. London was certainly a centre for the *wholesale* traffic in used clothing with buyers coming from different parts of the United Kingdom. That there was a good deal of foreign trade is borne out by the known export of bales of clothes and carpets to Belgium, France and specifically to Holland, and later, America[21]. A traveller towards the end of the 18th century wrote that the poorer class wandered through the streets of London, calling old clothes "which they buy up and mostly send abroad"[22], and Solomon Joseph, a dealer in new and second-hand clothing, said he bought for colonial export[23]. Further proof of this type of trade is apparent from the existing evidence, for though immigrants were not welcome in England, merchants were. In 1776 a certain Jacob Schloss of Frankfurt was advised to bring a proper passport with him as Parliament had brought in a new law, as well as a health certificate. Above all, he was told that he should say he was a *merchant travelling* to buy goods[24]. Other merchants, who came from France, were Lazarus Jacobs[25] and Samuel Wolf Oppenheimer from Paris. The latter stayed at Bevis

19. *ELM*, The Neighbourhood of Rag Fair (London, 1849).
20. *Times* 15/2/1832.
21. Lipman, *Social History*, p.33
22. Wendeborn, vol. II, p. 471.
23. OSBP, 1898-1899, p. 27.
24. Dushinsky, Letter dated 1776, pp. 103, 229-30.
25. Endelman, p. 178.

Marks and sold all sorts of Dutch toys and haberdashery[26]. David Samuel, "A Jew Merchant", said he sent a box of watches abroad which had been made for the foreign market. The box contained a hundred watches, some three cases and some two, and some with enamelled landscapes[27]. Other merchants used to have contracts with hospitals, public companies and large hotels to buy up all their worn-out linen which they then sold to the lint-makers at a good profit[28].

Somewhere between the poor immigrant hawkers and the rich merchants, there was another type of hawker such as Bashim Cherif Salim Ben Ali, stated to be an Indian, but more likely Arab, a licensed hawker. He imported carpets and tablecloths with him from his country to sell in the streets of England[29].

A criminal case against John Lipman in 1867 gives much information on the practices and extent of the Clothes Exchange at that time[30]. There were great quantities of clothes sold in the Exchange, thousands of pounds changing hands every day, with two or three thousand people buying and selling. The variety of size in the deals is remarkable. One witness, John Philips, when asked "You say the prisoner is not an extensive dealer?" replied, "Well he buys a coat for 9d and sells it for 1s. the same as I would do, I have known him buy as many as forty coats at a time, I have known him buy old white coats for 2d a piece, and I have known him buy large quantities of things at sales and likewise in the market". And he adds, "There are a few large dealers and some large firms and some small ones; you can buy a pair of trousers for 9d there".

There were in the market as well as the usual second-hand material, some quantities of new coats and trousers bought from the wholesalers after stocktaking or bought at auction;

26. CAT 1956 p. 60, note 427.
27. OBSP, 1784-1785, p. 344.
28. *Leisure*, July 1950, p. 491.
29. OBSP, 1896-1897, 12th Session, p. 879.
30. OBSP, 1867-1868 p.192 ff.

and also new, but slightly soiled goods, much of these being sold in bales.

One point on which there was general consensus was that no names, addresses or questions were asked about any goods on offer. The reasons given for this vary, but seem to come under the heading of 'accepted practice'. Elizabeth Aaron, a forthright and articulate woman, was in the unusual position for one of her sex of being a general dealer on the Exchange with clients all over the world. She said in evidence "We buy every day from persons who come to us, I never ask questions of people who buy things. I buy them in public market and give a fair price, it is not the first time I have bought new goods in the market" (i.e. it is not unusual or necessarily criminally obtained). And she added "I have bought from persons I did not know, during the day some things will change hands two or three times. If a man has goods I thought were right (e.g. not stolen) and that would suit me to get interest on, I should buy them. It is usual in the market to purchase of a person you don't know and without asking questions — you don't get the address of a person unless you go to a warehouse where you buy a large quantity of a stranger. I am not aware it is usual to ask questions, I never adopt that course". In reply to the Prosecutor's remark, "But you said just now you would not buy of a stranger?" Elizabeth Aaron replied, "Not if I thought they were not right — I would not buy off a child," and added she refused goods some days ago which were offered by a young man. John Adams confirmed this, "Unless we entertain suspicions we do not make enquiries of persons who bring things to sell"; and Joseph Phillips said, "We are not supposed to take an invoice of everybody that comes into the market or we should have to take hundred a day, because we buy and sell to a neighbour a minute afterwards". Further to this, Joseph, who had been an old clothes dealer for many years, assured the court that "sometimes a man brings in a whole bale of clothes and sells them, I should buy a party without any questions, I would buy five hundred coats of a man if he brought them in the public market, they are all exposed for sale and everybody is supposed to buy as cheap as they can without any question at all".

Joseph Adams gave another answer to the question, "I suppose you generally know the persons you buy large quantities from?" "No, we do not ask the person's name or have any receipt, we are all known to each other by sight, we get things as cheap as we can". This is followed by the possibly prejudiced, but even more categoric remarks of Joseph Lipman (a cousin of the accused). "If a man comes in with a bale of coats or trousers and sells them openly in the market, it is not thought necessary to ask who he is, where he comes from, or whether he has paid for them." The insistence of all the witnesses that the goods in question were for sale in the public market, probably indicates they were aware of the ancient law of *marché ouvert*, which states that a person selling goods in an open, legal, market and also in some pubs, cannot be accused of being a receiver of those articles even if they prove to have been stolen[31]. The general drawing together of the dealers in defence of their colleagues rings true. Nevertheless there may have been less acceptable reasons for the undemanding practices of the market.

As well as the wholesale department, there was a busy and profitable retail trade at Isaac's Exchange where there were separate stalls for retail buyers, let out at 3s per stall on Sundays, 2s on other days. There were said to be five or six hundred sellers and about a thousand buyers from all over London who made the exchanges and the surrounding streets almost impassable[32]. On Sundays, when the streets, though not the exchanges, were most crowded, there were many thieves[33]. A contemporary ballad in which a country boy describes Rag Fair, warns buyers to look after their purses because there are pickpockets about[34]. Isaac Ahronsberg was attacked in an alley off petticoat Lane where there were, he said, seven or eight hundred thieves in the middle of the road[35]!

31. J. Smouha, personal communication.
32. MILLS, pp. 268-9.
33. MILLS, p. 268.
34. *Eph*, The Humours of Rag Fair.
35. OBSP, 1856-1857, p. 366.

However, John Mills said that Rag Fair was far more honourable than the bar of *The Eagle Tavern* or the counter of a gin palace[36], and a French visitor in 1842 was of the opinion that the market Jews could not steal because they all knew each other; they live, he said on London's leavings[37]. On other days articles were rarely lost and it was generally known as a very honest place where things could, perhaps, pass (legally) through as many as twenty hands in one morning[38].

In this retail trade the clothes could either be re-sold as they were, or repaired and renovated, or made into other garments. The two latter possibilities were known technically as *clobbering* and some of the hawkers' wives and daughters undertook it. Otherwise the clothes were done up by keepers of poor coffee-houses and were occasionally bought by chandlers, low hairdressers and others. Levi Nathan's dream was to go out buying old clothes, whilst Mrs. Parry renovated them and "minded the shop"[39].

An eighteenth century traveller says there was very little clothing manufactured for the poor or common people and what was, was not liked and hardly ever seen, even in the country. He said people did their best to look well dressed and if they could not afford new, bought old at secondhand so that they could have "at least the appearance of finery"[40].

One old clothes man used to buy Chelsea Pensioners' clothes. They were given a new suit each year, but some of them managed to do up and re-button part of their old suits, and sell part of the new. When the governors heard of this, they gave orders for the men to receive their new suit only when the old one was handed over.

36. MILLS, p. 271.
37. FAUCHER, p. 33.
38. OBSP, 1844-1845, p. 416.
39. NATHAN, p. 5.
40. WENDEBORN, vol. I, p. 115.

These were then cut in pieces and sold to Mr. Rolson, a paper merchant[41].

A Jew, who may have been a certain Benjamin Harris who was licensed to buy wearing apparel of the soldiers at the barracks[42], and his three sons, went to see Mr. Rolson and agreed a price for the pieces. They bought patterns with them and fitted them to the pieces, sorting out what was useful and discarding the rest. They paid Mr. Rolson well, and as the cloth was only good for coarse paper, he was pleased. On asking them what they would do with the pieces, they replied that they had a shop in Houndsditch and would sell *new* holiday suits for the children of the poor, made from old Pensioners' clothes[43].

The treatment given to the various clothes in the market depended on their type and state. Mayhew gives a long detailed list of the clothing to be found, and some interesting points are repeated here.

Coats (all the better for being protected by grease!) could have new collars and cuffs and be relined with silk or something like it. If the sleeves were worn underneath the cloth could be matched, cut away, and replaced, and if the seams showed white with wear, they were coloured with a mixture of logwood and copperas (iron sulphate) so that poor men who could not afford to pay £5 or £6 for a new coat could, instead of wearing *slop*, look very well in a clobbered one[44]. If the coats were too old to be smartened, they were cut up and made into caps[45]; old frock coats were more useful than dress coats for this, as more caps could be produced from them[46]. All the caps both in the east and west end of London were at one time supplied by Polish Jews. Other coats were made into gaiters for poor country clergymen, or for clerks on a low income who could thus

41. PYNE, p. 242ff.
42. OBSP, 1819-1820, p. 197.
43. PYNE, p. 242.
44. MAYHEW, *London*, vol. II, p. 29.
45. Ibid.
46. Mrs. D. Alexander, personal communication.

"have their legs cased in fine broadcloth on a Sunday morning and vie with their betters in appearance at one third of the price"[47]; and cheap boot-makers also used the cloth for the legs of women's cloth boots[48]. The smaller pieces were made into spatter-dashes, very necessary in London's muddy streets. Waistcoats had the worn edges cut away, fancy buttons replaced the old ones, the buttonholes were re-made and the garment sold a size smaller than it was originally. Sometimes these too were made into cloth caps. (One social investigator in the 19th century, amongst other criteria, judged the status of a street by whether the children there wore boots and hats.)[49] Generally speaking the more flimsy, flashy, velvet and silk waistcoats were tidied up and sold as they were. Trousers were re-seated and repaired, or if the knees were worn, were cut short for boy's use[50].

There were more women's than men's clothes for sale[51]. Women's silk dresses were often sold as they were, or else cut down in size so as to remove the worn parts. If they were too worn they were made into little girls' jackets, or re-used for lining bonnets and muffs, or for the inside of book bindings. Black silk dresses were cut up to line coats. Most buyers liked to buy cotton, rather than silk dresses as they could be washed and starched to look almost like new. Under-clothes were patched and mended, though sometimes they were left as they were, as wives thought they must be cheaper in that state, and could be mended by themselves[52].

In the eighteenth century coats were often 'turned' that is, they were undone and re-made, the worn outside becoming the inside, and the less worn inside becoming the outside. This had rather gone out of fashion by the nineteenth century, although as late as 1827 old clothes men bought closely brushed coats for half-a-crown, which

---

47. PYNE, p. 249.
48. MAYHEW, *London*, vol. II, p. 29.
49. BOOTH, *Notebooks*, B (250), p.55, B (352), p.51, B (351), p. 185.
50. MAYHEW, *London*, vol. II, p. 29.
51. MILLS, p. 267.
52. MAYHEW, *London*, vol. II, p. 33, and note.

(after being turned and cleaned) gave a twenty per cent profit[53]. Trousers were rarely 'turned'[54].

'Wrack', or 'wrappers', or 'bale stuff', which was the coarse outer packaging of new goods, was bought wholesale and cut up by the street traders to make towels and aprons. They paid 1 ½ pence the lb for it, and it was said to bleach very well after a few washings[55]. Some of the absolutely unusable rags were turned into manure. A Swedish botanist on a visit to England in 1748 was told by farmers at Ivinghoe, thirty-four miles from London, that they regularly bought rags of all sorts from tailors and other people in London. They cut the rags up, strewed them over the wheat fields and ploughed them in before sowing. They said it was excellent manure, which amongst its other advantages, held moisture for a long time and "advanced the growth of crops"[56].

One very good market was in men's old silk hats. The hawkers would crush them a little to see if they were well made, and not too worn round the crown[57]. If the underlying form was good they could be re-blocked and re-covered with silk or velvet, as otherwise they were apt to disintegrate in the rain. One man who stood at the corner of Bishopsgate to catch the old clo' men on the way to the Exchange, bought up all the hats he could lay hands on, it was said up to thirty dozen a week![58] In 1810 Isaac Cardozo, having stolen sixty-eight hats, put them in his bag and offered forty-two of them for sale at 10d each — which was the right price for common felt hats in

53. PYNE, p. 249.
54. Mrs Debina, personal communication.
55. MAYHEW, *London*, vol. I, p. 30.
56. P. KALM, *Visit to England on his way to America*, tr. J. LUCAS, (London, 1892), p. 265.
57. BOOTH, *Life*, vol. III, p. 36.
58. BOOTH, *Life*, vol. III, p. 28.

a rough state[59]. By 1906 sellers of hats were usually the manufacturers themselves[60].

It is interesting to note that the hawkers seemed to judge the articles as much by touch as by sight. One of them explained that he could not only tell how long a coat had been worn by the feel of it, but in certain cases also tell the life-style of the wearer: a worn back denotes a gentleman; a worn left elbow and right arm, an author; worn under the left arm shows a left-handed wearer and so on[61]. Certainly the Jews in general were deeply interested in clothes and "it was common for them to examine each other's clothes". A Mr. Silvester says that he and Michael Levy were standing in a pub discussing whether another's friend's red waistcoat was made of Kerseymere or Beaver, so noticed nothing that was going on around them![62]

The second-hand trade in old boots and shoes merits a description of its own. This is sometimes said to have been the most lucrative part of the old clo' man's trade — as one remarked to Booth "There's nothing so saleable as a pair of old boots to us — I can sell a pair of old boots going along the streets if I carry them in my hand — the snobs will run after me to get these — the back are so valuable"[63]. But on the contrary another hawker says that they are the most difficult things to purchase in the whole old clothes business as unless they are absolutely sound they are not worth carrying home — "are just good for cutting up". Most boots, he continues, are bought to be re-sold to working men's clubs[64].

In a dust yard, a kind of rubbish dump, opening on to the Regent's Canal, there was a huge "black gulf, broad, wide and of unknown depth, filled within a few feet of the floor's surface with old shoes and boots". When the proprietor was asked of what use they

59. OBSP, 1820-1821, p. 350.
60. SIMS, p. 318.
61. AUSTIN, Letter XI, p. 67.
62. OBSP, 1789-1790, p. 318.
63. BOOTH, *Life*, vol. III, p. 28.
64. BOOTH, *Life*, vol. III, p. 28.

were, he replied that he sold them to the Jews as "they knows better what to do with 'em than we do, mister"[65]. And indeed they did. They were taken to Monmouth Street, which was the centre of the second-hand shoe trade to be 'translated'. This was, "to take a worn, old pair of shoes or boots and by repairing them make them appear as if left off with hardly any wear". This was obtained by rather dubious methods[66].

> Old Clothes — old clothes — old clo'
> Old Clothes is loudly crying.
> The old clothes man for bargains trying.
> This trade is practised by the Jews
> Who profit make from our old shoes.[67]

Articles which were too worn for the market or even for the pawnbrokers were taken to 'leaving' or 'dolly' shops. Here a man might buy a new coat from a week's entire wages, *leave* it immediately for a loan, and take it out on Sunday, return it for a smaller loan until gradually it came into his possession[68].

There is a contemporary description of a combined general and leaving shop at the corner of Hinton Street, Bethnal Green, where people went instead of going to a pawnbrokers. There were bundles of people's possessions all around, which were left as pledges for a day or a week; and the owners had the advantage of being able to choose either food or money in exchange[69]. Another shop of the same type belonged to the Tannenbaums. He was a provision dealer, while she lent money on goods. H. Barber sold them coats, trousers and a vest, all of which he had bought second-hand and repaired; and

65. GREENWOOD, *Journeys*, p. 64.

66. But Mayhew (*London*, vol. II, p. 34) says there were no Jews in Monmouth Street.

67. HINDLEY, *Cries*, p. 158.

68. GREENWOOD, *Journeys*, p. 15; CHESNEY, pp. 191-2.

69. OBSP, 1851-1852, p. 104.

Hannah de Wild bought a dress for 5s on the Exchange at Cutler Street and sold it to Mrs. Tannenbaum for 2s in silver and 2s in provisions[70].

From the eighteenth century onwards hawkers not only sold their goods to dealers in the Exchanges, but also in Rosemary and Petticoat Lanes. Although Rosemary Lane was the wider of the two streets, it was Petticoat Lane which attracted more customers as it consisted of many small side streets as well as a main street. Both these markets obtained most of their wares from the Exchange and were, in a sense, an extension of them. They were also a market for outlying districts beyond the neighbourhood of Tower Hill. Here there were sellers of second-hand clothes, and many household articles as well, all the way along the streets for three miles or more. Some of the goods such as boots and shoes, were piled up, with men's and women's old clothes on the pavements, some on barrows, or slung on clothes horses; or thrust into baskets[71]. Some were in tiny shops where the clothes were hung on wooden poles, or piled on chairs outside the door, or hung on railings below the first floor windows[72]. The roads were littered with casks and bags and bundles "from the fashionable bonnet shapelessly crushed, but still brilliant, to mildewed castors, boots, and slip-shod dancing shoes"[73].

One description says the casements of the houses on either side of these narrow streets were removed in hot weather and goods were displayed in the rooms, so that "the street forms a kind of channel between the apartments, as though this were one great family house"[74]. Another observer of the same phenomenon speaks of miles of streets where the houses' living rooms had the windows removed

70. OBSP, 1878-1879, p. 500.
71. JOSEPH, p. 10.
72. MAYHEW, *London*, vol.IV, p. 373.
73. GREENWOOD, *Journeys*, p. 57.
74. MAYHEW, *London*, vol. I, p. 37.

and were packed with merchandise — so that he wondered how the proprietors could get in or out![75].

The district of the Lane was quiet till after mid-day, but particularly busy on Sunday mornings. A description in 1897 says Wentworth Street was thronged with stalls, and buyers and sellers were nearly all Jews. The women were without hats, and wore wigs (as was the custom for Orthodox Jews in Eastern Europe) and had coarse woollen shawls over their shoulders. The market had more the appearance of a foreign scene than an English one[76], was said to be "one of the wonders of London, a medley of strange sights, strange sounds and strange smells. Streets crowded as to be thoroughfares no longer, and lined with a double or treble row of hand barrows, set fast with empty cases so as to assume the guise of market stalls"[77]. There was so much waste in the quarter, more rag pickers were to be found there than anywhere else in London[78].

The atmosphere of the Lane, described as a dirty street, was a lively one, with men calling their wares with cries such as "Breeches Folks", "Shoe Folks" and "Breaking Tailors"[79]; and shop-keepers urging possible buyers, more or less physically into the houses[80]. One writer remarks on "the tormenting importunities of the barking shop-keepers still permitted, as all can witness as they pass through Monmouth Street, Rosemary Lane, Houndsditch and Moorfields"[81].

75. SIMS, p. 17. During his trial for allegedly stealing silk, a witness said "Solomon Nathan is a general dealer - he has no shop, there is a room you may call a shop - but it is a private house - things hang up in the window: OBSP, 1833-34, p. 605.
76. BOOTH, *Notebooks*, B (182), p. 109, B (351), p. 40.
77. BOOTH, *Life*, vol. I, p. 66.
78. MAYHEW, *London*, vol. II, p. 67.
79. HUGHSON, p. 15.
80. AUSTIN, Letter XI, p. 67.
81. T.T. SMITH, *The Cries of London* (London, 1839).

The shopkeepers had a habit of accosting people who, if not interested in buying, were then asked if they wanted to *sell* any clothes. Both Austin and De Vega were asked if they would like to sell anything[82]. Sometimes the old clothes hawkers instead of going to the Exchanges, took their goods directly to the shops in Lane. There they would empty their bags onto the counter and be paid for the contents[83]. Although this was the usual method of sale when the Exchanges were not used, one shop keeper said he was very careful when hawkers came into the shop to show their goods, and preferred them to keep their bags outside[84]. There was also a good deal of bartering, but this was between sellers and had nothing to do with the public[85]. Amidst the general confusion there were young boys and girl pedlars selling oranges, lemons, nuts, cakes and drinks; and visitors strolling between the barrows — at night the whole scene lit up by flares.

By 1880 or 1890 the Lane had been taken over, literally, by Jewish vendors of old clothes and even some of the shop-keepers, who were a step above the street traders, were Jews. The street sellers always hoped to become shop owners but apparently seldom managed to do so, although some did work their way up. Ryland, a police commissioner, said he knew three or four who started with barrows and later had shops[86].

By 1897 the Lane had improved. It had become quite wide with a good pavement, and the market occupied "a large new thoroughfare lately opened", which "threatens to cross Commercial Street"[87]. That it became a thriving market is clear from various comments; remarks such as "There is probably no place in the world where people of all conditions may consult their circumstances so

---

82. AUSTIN, Letter XI, p. 67; DE VEGA, vol. I, pp. 13-4.
83. OBSP, 1844-1845, p. 416.
84. OBSP, 1783, p. 935.
85. OBSP, 1857-1858, p. 133.
86. BOOTH, *Notebooks*, B (352), Districts 9.6.5, p. 113.
87. *Jewish C.*, Nov. 9th, 1897.

effectually as in London"[88], or "It may be doubted if the Stock Exchange could exhibit more energy, vivacity, cupidity and tact as is here shown"[89], while Booth sums up as follows, "Petticoat Lane is the Exchange of the Jew, but the Lounge of the Christian"[90].

Certainly many aspects of Rag Fair were unattractive, but the ugly sights and smells were usual in the slums of the period. No worse, nor more degrading than the unwholesome hovels in which a great part of the public lived in unbelievable degradation and squalor.

The over-riding impression of the place and the surrounding streets is, however, one of extraordinary vitality. One has the feeling, when reading contemporary descriptions, of a scarcely contained excitement, a nervous tension, an exuberance which flowed against the narrow confines of the houses and imbued the most insignificant sale with a kind of magnificence.

88. SILLIMAN, vol. I, pp. 270-1.
89. *Knights Cyclopedia* (London), vol. I, 1851.
90. BOOTH, *Life*, vol. I, p. 66.

I. Private Collection

II. Guildhall Library and Art Collection

III. Luton Hoo Werner Collection

IV. Private Collection

V. Private Collection

VI. Burrell Collection, Glasgow

VII. Burrell Collection, Glasgow

VIII. Luton Hoo Werner Collection

IX. Luton Hoo Werner Collection

X. Jewish Museum, London

XI. Jewish Museum, London

XII. Metropolitan Museum, New York

XIII. Jewish Museum, London

RAGS AND BONES.

XIV. Private Collection

XV. (Private Collection)

XVI. Guildhall Library, London

CHAPTER V

LIFE STYLE AND CRIME

Before the introduction of the police force, the law in the streets was supposed to be upheld by old men known as "The Watch". They were armed with a wooden stick, or pole, and a rattle which they "sprung" to call for assistance. Their duties were to hit the house doors to see they were properly closed, and warn the proprietors if they were not, to cry the hours, tell the weather, and give 'notice of fires'[1]. In 1731 "the Winter Watch" in Manchester was warned that it had to be careful to recruit only able-bodied men[2]. There were also slightly more efficient, better paid men, called 'the Patrol'.

In one description of London (1789) it is said that there was a Watch House every hundred yards, containing a man with a gun and bayonet who was supposed to give the alarm by ringing a bell if he saw any suspicious person. This is only mentioned on one occasion and is possibly incorrect, although there is indeed one picture of a Patrol man with a bayonet. However, a French visitor in 1725 said London does not have *any* watchmen, either on foot or horseback, to prevent robberies — only a man to be seen in every street with a lantern and a stick![3]

Under these circumstances the number of thieves actually brought to court is astonishing. Very often they were caught by what today would be called 'Citizen's Arrest'. At the cry 'stop thief' almost anyone around would give chase, and there are many descriptions in criminal cases of exciting chases up and down the streets and alleys of London, with passers-by joining in to cut off the thief's escape and take him to the Watch House, the Patrol House or the Magistrates. Suspicious-looking characters were often stopped and questioned about where they were going, what goods they were

1. D'ARCHENHOLZ, vol. II, p. 75.
2. *Manchester Court Leet Records*, vol. III (Cheetham Library).
3. C. DE SAUSSURE, *A Foreign View of England in the Reigns of George I and George II* (London, 1725), p. 68.

8

carrying and so on; sometimes they ran away, or got into an argument, in which onlookers joined, and it generally finished with their arrest — occasionally of a bona fide hawker who had to prove his innocence in court.

Gambling, which old clothes men are often accused of, began in the hawkers' youth, with marbles played for 'Albert Rock' and 'Hardbake'. As adults they were specially fond of a game which consisted of tossing a three-farthing coin in the air and calling heads or tails. During a court case in 1755 a witness was seen to be tossing up halfpence![4] This was called 'one a time' as one shilling was bet on each toss. Other hawkers would surround the players and bet on the winner .... sometimes there was £30 in silver and gold on the ground whilst this game went on[5]. The old clothes men liked to play draughts and dominoes for money in the coffee houses round the Exchange and they had been known to wager fifty pounds, but only after great gambling gains[6]. On Saturdays they would play draughts or dominoes for the greater part of the afternoons. Even an admirer of their characteristics speaks of their favourite vice of gambling, and the hawkers would, indeed, readily gamble away a day's hard-won earnings — just because they loved to speculate.

The results of this weakness for gambling were often tragic. Old clothes dealer Moses Spencer fell in with some gamblers in Duke's Place, London, and began playing 'All Fours' for a shilling a game. When he had lost fourteen shillings he remembered his wife had just had a child, and rushed off to her sister to borrow half a guinea, hoping to win his money back. Losing all, ruined, he stole some clothes and finished up being transported[7]. Joseph Da Costa was tried for obtaining £13 from John White by an unlawful game of dice, called 'Hazard'[8]. Harry Levi, too, fell into trouble: he pawned his new

4. OBSP, 1755, p. 191.
5. MAYHEW, *London*, vol. II, p. 120.
6. MAYHEW, *London*, vol. II, p. 120.
7. OBSP, 1767-1768, p. 135.
8. OBSP, 1776-1777, p. 91.

buckskin breeches, and then gamed the money away in the Lottery Office. When he needed to wear the breeches to go out on his master's coach, he tried to sell some stolen harness to get enough money to retrieve them and found himself in court[9].

As one observer says, "gambling is a vice of the intellect"[10] and another notes, it is "a well-marked cause of destitution among the Jews"[11]. It seems to have been taken for granted by a committee member of the Jewish Association for the Protection of Women, who, speaking of a woman's husband, said "It is well known he is an inveterate gambler." The Chief Rabbi, Dr. Adler, when asked about gambling, made the rather hermetic remark that "the low type is not prevalent, but there is a good speculative temperament but this might not be of the nature of gambling"[12]. Booth also spoke of the Jewish passion for gambling[13]. When one considers their narrow, poverty-stricken, back-breaking work, it is not surprising the Old Clothes men indulged in the occasional extravagance, which the thrill of gambling gave them.

By 1900 at least twenty of the streets which in Booth's map of three years earlier were coloured black to indicate they were extremely poor and inhabited by semi-criminal, vicious people, had become Jewish and respectable[14].

The English Jews themselves often criticised, privately, their foreign brethren. Rabbi Stern of Stepney Causeway, said the foreigners were the culprits of prostitution, while the English Jews without a doubt were, as a rule, good. But the Reverend Burnet, seventy per cent of whose parish consisted of Jews, the bulk of whom were foreigners of the poorest class, stated that they were better tenants

---

9. OBSP, 1781-1782, p. 271.
10. BOOTH, *Life*, vol. I, p. 189.
11. BPP, *Board of Trade Commission on Alien Immigration 1894*, p. 53.
12. BOOTH, *Notebooks*, XXVII, B. 196/202.
13. BOOTH, *Life*, vol. III, p. 185.
14. BOOTH, *Notebooks*, 13 FB (351), p. 81; RUSSELL, p. 176.

than the English, as "somehow or other they pay, and they pay regularly"[15].

Most of the immigrants who took to hawking old clothes, or peddling, were described as uncouth, illiterate, narrow-minded and poor, and ignorant of the English language. That they were indeed uncouth, narrow-minded and poor, is irrefutable, but some of them were not illiterate[16]. A minority of Jewish boys would have had some education, though narrow in outlook they would at least have been able to read Hebrew and might have studied the Torah (five first books of the Old Testament) and possibly some commentaries. This trained their intellect, their memory and reasoning powers, and together with their industry and patience was often seen as the secret of their survival, and sometimes, success.

As well as those with minimum literacy there are many examples of highly-educated men amongst hawkers and pedlars. Levi Nathan was educated in Hamburg under Rabbi Jonathan, and on his way to England he preached in Germany, Italy and France[17].

Once installed, he supported his family in London by dealing in old clothes and by running a kind of religious club for the Synagogue, where he read and expounded the Bible to the members in the evenings, for which he was paid £30 a year[18]. Michael Simmons, dealer in old clothes, spoke of a society of this type which met from seven till nine in the evenings, where the members studied Jewish Law[19].

Levi was anxious for his children to be educated and sent them to Mrs. Parry, with whom he was in love, to learn English and Hebrew, the latter he had himself taught her. Later, he sent his

---

15. BOOTH, *Notebooks*, Misc. XLVI B. (225), p. 21.

16. PICCIOTTO, p. 93.

17. He probably preached in Yiddish, a lingua-franca amongst European Jews, except for Spanish and Portuguese Jews, who spoke Ladino, a kind of ancient Spanish.

18. NATHAN, p. 3.

19. OBSP, 1776-1777, p. 302.

daughter to a school run by Mrs. Parry, but by this time, having more or less quarrelled with him, she vented her anger on the poor child. She was badly treated and on one occasion came home with scratches all the way up her arms.

Levi ends his autobiography with a most touching description of his faithless love. The reader he says, "may perhaps be desirous before I take leave of him, that I should give some description of Mrs. Parry and her diabolical friend" (the lover who displaced him) .... "of the lady's person we will endeavour to say something. She is about thirty years of age, tall and genteel, of a sallow complexion, black eyes, dark hair and eyebrows, a little pug-nosed, dresses in the fashion, very well spoken can cry with one eye and laugh with the other as she one day showed me, is, (as the Prophet Jeremiah says of the human heart) deceitful above all things and desperately wicked"[20].

Other scholars included Jacob Kimhi, Joseph, who was "a bit of a wit" and well educated[21], Samuel Harris, a hawker from Germany who was sent to Hebrew school at the age of four and higher school at six[22]. Then there was Elijah Rabbinovitch who was "a Hebrew writer by choice and a pedlar by necessity"[23] and another old man, a seller or old clothes for fifty years, who spoke and wrote a dozen languages[24].

Morris Lissack was another well educated pedlar. An accomplished but boring writer, he came to England, circa 1839 and pawned his watch and some of his clothes to buy pedlars' goods. His first position was on London Bridge, where he stood in great embarrassment. He soon settled in Bedford, where he taught German, before becoming a jeweller and silver-smith, and later a wine and spirit merchant. He raised seven children and became trustee of a charity where he brought influence to bear for the Jews to be exempted from

20. NATHAN, p. 6.
21. FELIX, p. 20. For Kimhi see above Ch. II, 44
22. CLEGG, p. 6.
23. GARTNER, p. 59.
24. BOOTH, *Life*, vol. III, p. 32.

school attendance "on any days set apart for religious observance", on seven days notice[25].

Moses Emmanuel, a man of great learning, was a pedlar whose walk was in Leicestershire, where he was well known in the countryside. He used to spend a great deal of time with Mr. Caste, the Minister of the church at Hinckley, who was a scholarly man and "a master of every subject to which he applied himself". They discussed theological questions, chiefly the fifty-first and fifty-second chapters of Isaiah. The minister did his best to convince his friend of the truths of Christianity and the Jew received much pleasure from his conversation[26]. Zangwill describes the three-hatted scarecrow who shambled along snuffling "old clo'" as having an inner life of great intensity and elevation and even a sense of humour. He continues with the story of the pedlar in a country pub who being teased by the locals and asked where Moses was when the light went out, replied in Yiddish, translated by a bystander, that there was a perpetual light round Moses' head, so it could never go out[27]. A missionary to the Jews also noticed that men of shabby appearance doing menial work, such as hawking, were often men of no small mental culture[28].

On the other hand, lack of education was clearly perceived as a problem, particularly by some of the leaders of the community. A letter from an English Jew to the Paris Sanhedrin (Jewish legal council) said that Jewish children were sent out to earn their living at an early age, and asked how many old clothes men and vendors of oranges, slippers and shoe strings would be following more useful occupations had they had the advantage of more education. He suggested there would have been less profligacy and wretchedness to be seen in public places and streets if the children had received a

25. LISSACK, p. 66ff.; Bedford County Record Office, Morris Lissack, 1839, 1847, 1854, 1861, 1871.

26. J. NICHOLS, *Leicester History and Antiquities*, vol. III, Pt. I (London, 1780), p. 744.

27. ZANGWILL, p. 30.

28. *Church*, p. 14.

better education. It is not impossible that Frey, who was a missionary to the London Jews, fabricated this letter for his own ends. He quotes it in one of his own to the Missionary Society, insisting on greater facilities for teaching Jewish children with the ultimate aim of conversion[29]. However his ideas are not unlike those of a contributor to the *Jewish Chronicle*, who complained that the Jewish poor too easily put their children into trades where there was no future, and that what was required was better education[30].

Amongst the old clothes men's good points, sobriety is often mentioned with admiration and even disbelief. Drink was the solace, perhaps the only one, of the poorer classes of the eighteenth and nineteenth centuries — and also their downfall. A clergyman in Bethnal Green said a high proportion of the population was connected in one way of another with the buying, selling or serving of drinks, those who were not were Jews living in the better districts[31]. A medical officer states "Jews do not drink" and ascribed this to their "forms and ceremonies" which lead to a better home life"[32], and a policeman, who had spent three years in the poorest quarter of the East End, said he had not seen six Jews brought into the station drunk[33]. Another informant told Booth that "the Jew clothes man is seldom or ever seen in liquor," and when he did drink it was usually in the privacy of his club; and a missionary adds that it was very rare to find a Jew intemperate[34]. He might, however, occasionally be seen at a public house, enjoying a glass of 'Rum and Shrub', which Henry Gershon called for on the way to a deal[35], and James Hyatt kept a bottle of it in his great-coat pocket, which he said was "only a little

29. FREY, *in* Mission, p. 34.
30. *Jewish C.*, May 10th, 1872
31. BOOTH, *Notebooks*, B. District (182) 10 X L Bethnal Green, p. 1, B. (351), p. 87.
32. BOOTH, *Notebooks*, B. District (181), p. 14.
33. BOOTH, *Notebooks*, B. (351), p. 87
34. *Church*, vol. 1-3, p. 14.
35. OBSP, 1837-1838, p. 709.

shrub"[36]. Anderson said apologetically, that he only had rum and shrub because he felt cold and was "subject to taking cold"[37].

The drink which old clothes men really preferred was 'Kosher' rum, which was said to be extremely nourishing. Another observer said that though Jews drank a good deal they rarely, if ever, "fall victim to the passion for alcohol," and spent little on drink, but enjoyed a game of cards on a Saturday or Sunday evening, when they might fling money away on gambling[38].

Given the type of goods handled by the hawkers and pedlars, their extreme poverty, lack of knowledge of English ways, and being often surrounded by inimical neighbours, it is not surprising many old clothes men were without doubt engaged in crime, at least in a small way, as indeed were many members of the lower classes or 'mob'. By its nature the second-hand clothes trade would have had connections with criminals; robbers would have to go to the traders to dispose of their goods. The Jews who came from the ghettoes of Europe lived in the poorest part of London, and the East End had always been a centre for dealing in second-hand and stolen goods — so its bad reputation was thus not entirely the fault of the old clothes men[39]. One crime, it was said, in which the hawkers were involved was that they were bringing stolen goods into London from the sea ports, and the country, in one-horse carts. At best they may have failed to enquire very closely whence came some of their purchases — some bought at a price knowing well the goods must have been stolen, others may just have been negligent or even have innocently ignored their provenance[40]. One pickpocket remarked "Jews will buy anything

36. OBSP, 1819-1820, p. 273.
37. OBSP, 1830-1831, p. 50.
38. RUSSELL, p. 58.
39. As early as 1697 when hawkers were only allowed to trade in certain goods, among which was glass, they used to say they were glass traders and then hid the forbidden goods, such as linen, under the straw on which the glass was exposed.
40. COLQUHON, p. 49.

off you, but you must take their price". His particular wares were the handkerchiefs stolen from rich men's skirted coats. *Kingsmen* were the brightest coloured and most frequently stolen. Everyone knew where they came from, even the police[41]. But a bird catcher's wife, speaking of selling hare skins, said she always sold to Jews because she got better prices and "they buy readier"[42]. In any case, if the sellers kept their wits about them they got fair prices[43].

Some of the old clothes men had connections with wandering Jews on the Continent, who went from village to village collecting skins for the leather trade and who did not have a very good reputation[44]. They may have been part of those known as Betteljuden, who were wanderers on the roads, owing to the limitations on trades Jews were allowed to follow [45].

The magistrate, Colquhon, who from his profession must have known the truth about what was going on, accused the Jews of the increase in petty crime and suggested that the old clothes dealers should be licensed. He accused the hawkers "under the pretence of hawking old clothes" of "holding out temptation to servants to pilfer and steal vast quantity of bed linen, table linen, and old clothes in private families"[46], though an equally well-informed, but a later investigator stated that Jews never removed anything from houses they visited. This was not, however, always the case as Samuel Isaacs, old clothes man, could not resist taking two hats that were hanging in the hall of a house he was visiting; and running off down the street with them[47].

The magistrate went on to say that Jews acquired property and became receivers of stolen goods. Receivers generally

41. MAYHEW, *London*, vol. III, p. 382.
42. MAYHEW, 'Survey', vol. II, p. 62.
43. PYNE, p. 242.
44. ENDELMAN, p. 176.
45. J. JACOBS, *Jewish Statistics* (London, 1891), p. 36.
46. COLQUHON, p. 72.
47. OBSP, 1789-1790, p. 378.

lived in Somers Town, Spitalfields, Phillips Buildings and Rosemary Lane, all old clothes hawkers' areas, particularly the two latter. A polemicist said there were twenty-five receivers in Worship Street and one hundred and twenty-six in Marlborough Street![48] A list of goods found at a receiver's, belonging to fourteen different people, included every type of object from a hundred and fifty-six Persian goat skins to a case of surgical instruments![49]

Dealers lived like the poor around them and some, although in reality quite rich, had a very battered appearance[50]. Unlike the street sellers, their business was a mystery, "they also deal in stolen goods and in altering base money" and were said to have had "a capacity for silent evasion of the law, a faculty for secretive and illicit dealing"[51]. Writing in 1821 Mainwaring said, "the very soul and being of their traffic are secrecy, confidence and every wicked contrivance which the most subtle and refined craft can produce"[52]. There is a distinction between the dealers, receivers and the old clothes men who often supplied them, which did not always seem to be recognized.

Trials at the Old Bailey between 1745 and 1900 show Jews in every type of crime, from murder (extremely rare) down to petty thieving, and even, in one case, smuggling[53]. There are, of course, varying opinions as to the number of Jews, and hawkers and pedlars amongst them, who were participating in crime. A mid-eighteenth century merchant, who was certainly prejudiced (he subscribed to a petition against the Naturalization Bill) said Jews consist of hawkers, pedlars and traffickers, particularly those dealing in stolen goods, and not infrequently in coining. And D'Archenholz, on his tour of England, agreed with him. He said "the Jews who quit

48. MAINWARING, p. 87.
49. OBSP, 1853-1854, p. 711.
50. BOOTH, *Conditions*, p. 25.
51. BOOTH, *Life*, vol. I, p. 181.
52. MAINWARING, p. 87.
53. OBSP, 1827-1828, p. 511.

Holland and Germany take refuge in England, where they live by roguery, and even if they did not steal, help to conceal and dispose of the plunder"[54]. Southey also said the Jews, while ostensibly trading in old clothes, dealt also in stolen goods[55]. But D. George explains it was their exclusion from industry and their desperate poverty coupled with the multiplication of the number of pedlars "to a point at which it was impossible for them all to gain a living" which drove them to receiving goods[56].

It seems, as usual, there were differing opinions about the hawkers' involvement in crime. The comment of the Commission of the Board of Trade on Alien Immigration (1894) that "It may be stated generally that the evidence shows the amount of crime traceable to this class of immigrants is probably less rather than greater than the normal proportion among the whole population of London", is of great importance bearing in mind that this was a reputable and unprejudiced body[57].

It was in the eighteenth century that the elders of the community grew alarmed at the possibly exaggerated part the Dutch Jews played in crime. The Great Synagogue offered a reward for information about stolen goods, and in 1766 passed on information to the Bow Street Magistrate, Sir John Fielding, who wrote to the Communities' presidents as follows: "thinks himself much obliged to them, as is the public for the assistance they have already given to the civil power to detect the receivers of stolen goods in Duke's Place, Houndsditch, etc"[58]. In 1771 men responsible for a brutal murder were excommunicated by the Synagogue, and the wardens visited the Lord Mayor, who offered a free pass to any Jew who wanted to leave

54. D'ARCHENHOLZ, vol. I, p. 180.
55. SOUTHEY, p. 396.
56. GEORGE, p. 12.
57. BPP, *Board of Trade Commission on Alien Immigration 1894*, p. 61.
58. WOLF, MS.

England and return to their former home; it is pretty certain none took advantage of the offer[59].

Twenty-five years later an eminent Jew wrote a series of letters in which he drew up a plan to encompass all the needs of the poor — and thus reduce the crime rate among them. But friction between sections of a divided Jewish community prevented its implementation; if it had come into being, the arrangements for funding would have resulted in Jews being taxed under a system differing from the rest of the British public![60]

There does seem to have been a good deal of unorthodox buying and selling amongst the dealers themselves and some Jews were known fences, such as the receiver Isaac Judah[61], and Mrs. Sherwood of Bowl Yard St Giles[62]. Moss Benjamin, who was a witness in a trial, said the prisoner to his knowledge had been a receiver for fifteen or twenty years[63]. Another receiver known as "Moses" came downstairs at three o'clock in the morning to let in two thieves, and when offered some clothes and Prussian blue, stolen from a ship, promptly bought the goods for four guineas — and no questions asked[64]. Levy Levy, who was sorting rags which he bought for his own account, saw Elias Mordecai show two strangers, at their request, into a back room. Mordecai then bought three glasses (coach windows), a bridle, a cloth coat, and a carpet, all stolen, for two and a half guineas, and passed the lot on to his brother to sell[65]. Michael Simons, the old clothes man, bought a coat for half-a-crown in the parlour of a public house, and arranged to buy a saddle, a pair of harness and three coach glasses the next day, knowing full well they

59. ROTH, *Synagogue*, p. 159.
60. ROTH, *History*, p. 236ff.
61. RUMNEY, p. 71.
62. OBSP, 1802-1803, p. 535.
63. OBSP, 1861-1862, p. 469.
64. OBSP, 1786-1787, p. 666.
65. OBSP, 1791-1792, p. 66.

must have been stolen goods[66]. Though he is quoted as insisting on his honesty (p. 109)

Asher Cohen tells how a man brought some silver into his shop saying "Mr. Cohen, I must have £30." So Asher looked in the bag, went upstairs and brought the money. "I had bought all sorts of things from Mr. Cropper, I am a pretty general dealer — they were only fit for melting down!" Asher later explained[67]. And Samuel Mecum, who sold goods he had bought to Samuel Levi, another old clothes man, was asked in a court case if he had ever sold stolen goods before, replied "Yes, several times," and he had dealt with "a hundred thieves"; but a witness said Mecum "took a deal of pains to get his living by buying old clothes"[68].

Stolen goods could change hands at considerable speed. Isaiah Israel, asked what his business was, replied "I am a dealer in old clothes" and questioned "Is it common in your business to buy and sell to each other?" answered "Yes, very common." When the court enquired how long some stolen goods were in his possession, he replied "not above five minutes, I went with some of the things to Rag Fair, and sold them there, and this coat and breeches I sold to a tailor in Houndsditch who deals in old clothes, and I sold the other things to different people, but this coat and breeches and another coat I sold the same day, a few minutes after I bought them"[69].

In what appears to have been an equally quick succession of buying and selling, Aaron Lazarus, "I am in the watch line," indicted for receiving, said that he bought a watch from Smith for three pounds five shillings and sold it to Levi "the Clobberer" for three pounds six shillings and he sold it to Charles Hoppe for four pounds fifteen. Lazarus indignantly denied it was the same watch as he said, and one believes him, that he would never have sold a watch for three pounds six shillings for which he could get four pounds

---

66. OBSP, 1776-1777, p. 302.
67. OBSP, 1791-1792, p. 237.
68. OBSP, 1744-1747, p. 138.
69. OBSP, 1784-1785, p. 409.

fifteen. Finally, Hoppe sold the watch to Caesar Long, and it was stolen from *him* by two young unknown women who walked arm-in-arm with him down the street for a little way[70]. In further quick sales Penell Wolf bought a stolen coat, breeches, great coat, and several other articles for three pounds ten at eleven o'clock and had sold them all by two or three![71] Likewise Israel Davis bought a hat in suspicious circumstances and sold it again ten minutes later to a shop in Monmouth Street[72]. Philip Abrahams was quick to rid himself of thirteen yards of stolen silk, giving it to his sister, who gave it to a woman who sold it to a pawnbroker. "Does not the prisoner deal in buying and selling old clothes?" he was asked during his trial for stealing, and Abrahams described how he was walking along crying 'old clothes' when a man called him and sold him the silk. The truth of the matter was, he had stolen a box containing the silk, pease, snuff, beans and parcels of seeds which had been left outside *The George* at Snowhill, to be sent to Wales[73]. Lewis Levick, a dealer in shawls, made haste too, to sell some stolen ones. He never minded how he got them and when asked if he would buy from anybody without enquiring where the goods came from, said "We buy many in that way"[74]. And when a Mr. Cook was asked how he came by five yards of stolen woollen cloth, declared "it was none of his" and that Morris gave it to him to carry to Duke's Place to sell it to the Jews [75].

Charles Cowen's defence, on trial for stealing, has a familiar ring: "I am a Jew, I travel with a box, I had been at Barnet, I was very tired — so I got up behind this wagon, and when it started I fell down, and this (the stolen box) fell down on top of me"[76].

70. OBSP, 1827-1828, p. 84.
71. OBSP, 1784-1785, p. 409.
72. OBSP, 1786, p. 865.
73. OBSP, 1751-1755, p. 95.
74. OBSP, 1816-1817, p. 176.
75. OBSP, 1768-1769, p. 251.
76. OBSP, 1781-1782, p. 630.

But others were more selective when buying goods, and refused to be drawn into crime. Simon Isaacs was dismayed when a man brought someone to him who was looking for three stolen cushions, "You know I never buy anything of the sort"[77], he said, and Michael Alexander, when offered a stolen pot, stated he did not want to buy such things[78]. Moses Emmanuel, when offered two stolen spoons, said "I am an old clothes man, I do not buy such"[79]. While Michael Simons said *he* dealt in coach glasses, clothes and "everything that is honest"[80].

Old clothes men were occasionally involved in breaking and entering. Francis Levy, indicted for burglary, said he dealt in old clothes[81]; and Jacob and Angel Levy were taken to Court to explain their possession of 32 lbs of wool which had been burgled. Garrulous Jacob, "I have a great deal to say for myself", was crying 'old clothes' when a seafaring man called him into a public house and offered him wool at nine pence the pound. "I offered him sixpence and gave him sevenpence," he continued and quickly sold the lot for eightpence the pound, but was unable to get paid because he was afraid to touch money on the Sabbath [82]. Another Jacob, answering a jocular friend who thought all Jews refused to touch money on that day, retorted "as to money, or a pretty girl, they may be touched at any time!"[83]

But at least in the early days the occasional burglaries were almost comic in their ineptitude, as in the case of Levi Wolf, who said Joseph Elias, known as "Joe, the old clothes man", asked him to lend him and Solomon Gabrial a ladder, which he did. Elias and Gabrial took the ladder and lent it up against a wall to get into Benjamin da Costa's house. Gabrial stayed below, not a very useful

77. OBSP, 1790-1791, p. 575.
78. OBSP, 1798-1799, p. 429.
79. OBSP, 1764-1766, p. 15.
80. OBSP, 1776-1777, p. 302.
81. OBSP, 1817-1818, p. 73.
82. OBSP, 1786-1787, p. 549.
83. OBSP, 1762-1764, p. 208.

accomplice as he was "too stiff and clumsy" to climb it, so Gabrial helped shove and pull it up and over to the other side. When they found they couldn't get it back to Levi, he said if he told his master he would be transported, so they gave him some money and advised him to go peddling in the country[84].

As time went on burglaries became more common and on occasion quite rich hauls were made. Abraham Davis, a traveller who had been in the business for twelve years, had his box stolen from his room, whilst he was in the coffee house where he spent his evenings. It contained:

30 gold rings	
24 gold breast shirt buckles set with pearls	£ 19.10s
68 silver watches,	£119.10s
30 gold breast buckles set with garnets,	£ 6.10s
36 gold breast shirt buckles,	£ 7.10s
30 gold rings set with precious stones,	£ 15.10s
18 gold rings set with garnets,	£ 5.10s
18 pairs silver shoe buckles	£ 19.13s
1 leather pocket book,	. 2s
All in a wooden box,	. 2s[85]

Amongst smaller thefts there seems to have been a good deal of pickpocketing at the Bank, the Royal Exchange, and Jews Walk, the proceeds in notes being disposed of in Holland[86]. The young pedlar boys were also accused of altering base silver, which they bought up at a low price when it became too base to circulate, whitening it and sending it out again under the cover of selling oranges.[87]

84. OBSP, 1751-1755, p.67.
85. OBSP, 1778, p. 17.
86. G. PARKER, *A View of Society and Manners* (London,1781), p. 142.
87. SOUTHEY, p. 396.

Hyman Moses, who was selling oranges on Christmas Day, was indicted for passing a counterfeit shilling in change. The shilling was "merely coloured, not plated" and he landed in gaol for six months as a result[88]. Gadaliah Phillips, old clothes man, was selling peaches when *he* gave a counterfeit seven shilling piece in change. He had one guinea, two halfpennies and two seven shilling coins on him, all bad![89]

However, Colquhon said the Jews were only interested in copper and that counterfeit shillings were sold by tradesmen at threepence each, and a constable remarked "we called in some Jews to sell some bad shillings"[90]. Nearly sixty years later a police officer said Abraham Atkins made his living by selling counterfeit coins in the street, so there may have been a grey area where this was accepted practice[91].

What might, in some cases appear to be occasional small crimes, such as the stealing of pewter pots from pubs, or the tops of basement railings, were in reality a criminal's speciality[92]. John Harris was caught with not only a pot in his pocket, but a basket containing six more belonging to different publicans[93]. Chapman had a quart pot in one pocket and a pint in the other[94]. Henry Goldsmith stole four pewter pots from two different people[95], while Thomas Deema went one better and stole three pots from three people[96]. Even Isaac Israel, aged eighty-two, who said he was "a poor old man as lame as a cricket", managed to steal a pewter pot![97] This may explain

88. OBSP, 1812-1813, pp. 138-9

89. OBSP, 1805-1806, p. 87.

90. OBSP, 1791-1792, p. 127.

91. OBSP, 1861-1862, p. 92.

92. MAYHEW, *London*, vol. IV, pp. 25-6; OBSP, 1837-1838, pp. 294, 330, 684.

93. OBSP, 1805-1806, p. 332.

94. OBSP, 1806-1807, p. 123.

95. OBSP, 1849-1850, p. 614.

96. OBSP, 1820-1821, p. 91.

97. OBSP, 1808, p. 267.

the apparent differences in sentences, from fairly light to extremely severe, for what at first sight look like the same type of crime.

Pawnbrokers, whom one might have thought would be receivers, were, on the contrary, very careful about what they bought. They generally refused goods they suspected of being stolen, probably because they were more open to the law's surveillance[98]. James Bland tried to sell a stolen mould to four different pawnshops, who all refused him[99]. Sometimes they questioned a client, and if not satisfied would call an Officer[100]. James Jacobs said Peter Moss pawned clothes several times and as he thought him dishonest, asked him, the next time he came in, if they were his own clothes. When Moss said "No," Jacobs later strolled round into Rosemary Lane where he saw Moss serving in a clothes shop and realised he must be stealing the owner's stock[101]. The pawnbrokers were used to thieves' tricks and quickly noticed traces of a picked-out mark on a shirt[102], or a filed-out crest or initials on a watch[103]. One employee noticed a crest on some spoons offered to him and thought it was "not quite right, so stopped them"[104]. Joseph Clark sent for a policeman when he was offered books which, as he said, "You cannot have bought, for one certainly has not been finished"[105]. Another noticed a crest on some forks and referred to the Police List. This was a useful list detailing stolen goods[106]; *The Pawnbrokers' Gazette* carried similar descriptions[107]. If thieves had quantities of the same type of goods to dispose of, they sometimes sold small amounts to different pawnbrokers, so as not to arouse suspicion. Harry Ross obtained a

98. OBSP, 1820-1821, p. 6; 1821-1822, p. 75; 1825-1826, p. 587.
99. OBSP, 1846, p. 763.
100. OBSP, 1849-1850, p. 772.
101. OBSP, 1747-1749, p. 83.
102. OBSP, 1825-1826, p. 578; 1882-1883, p. 247.
103. OBSP, 1845-1846, p. 761.
104. OBSP, 1842, p. 1154.
105. OBSP 1863-1864, p. 154.
106. OBSP, 1869-1870, p. 177.
107. OBSP, 1893-1894, p. 431.

hundred and thirty-six tablecloths by false pretences, and pledged them at fifteen brokers[108].

Occasionally shops also recognized illegal goods. George Simmonds said a man brought two silver watches into his shop to ask about having the plates removed. The client returned the next day with the names on the plates obliterated. In the meantime Simmonds had received the Police List where the stolen watches appeared, and consequently retained them. He remarked, however, that it was not unusual to alter names on watches[109].

In spite of the immense difficulties the hawkers had to combat in their lives, there were very few adult criminals. There were, however, juvenile Jewish offenders. According to a police officer some young Jews were thieves, recidivists; because there was no Jewish Industrial School, the magistrates were reluctant to condemn boys of under fourteen to a reformatory, and so let them off. This had the effect of distorting the criminal figures[110]. But in earlier times many quite young children, eleven to fifteen year olds, were transported.

John Bebbington, sometime pedlar, gives eye witness accounts in his autobiography of the many tricks employed by men and women criminals, in comparison with which the old clothes men's crimes appear minimal, "but pursued, perhaps, with greater intelligence than their neighbours'"[111].

There is a perceivable change in crimes by Jews as the centuries advance. In the eighteenth century most of the crimes of thieving and receiving appear to be spur of the moment, taking of opportunities rather than planned crimes, though there were, as already stated, some professional receivers and criminals. There was an evolution as time went on, from petty thieving and occasional burglary, to more sophisticated crimes entailing complicated borrowing; forgery of anything from bills of exchange, orders for

108. OBSP, 1862-1863, p. 300.
109. OBSP, 1872-1873, p. 458.
110. BOOTH, *Notebooks*, B. 352, p. 49.
111. CHESNEY, p. 191.

goods, foreign notes (Russian) and even theatre tickets, as well as fraudulent financial practices, large-scale coining and more ambitious burglaries. Amongst small-times thieves, the snatching of handkerchiefs was replaced by the taking of watches dangling temptingly on chains across men's waistcoats. Copper coining was replaced by the making and passing of bad sixpences and shillings. The accused themselves are of a different type, no longer hawkers and pedlars, but small business men, or shop keepers, employees of large firms, or men engaged in financial dealings, bankrupts and so on. Many had anglicized their names so are more difficult to detect in the archives.

The thieves and receivers were more organized. "Their eyes are everywhere and they instantly know every movement in the criminal community before it is even seen by the public"[112]. There were special houses known as "plants", where goods purchased by a receiver could be stored till it was deemed safe to move them. The term was already in use in the eighteenth century. Abraham Nathan, a servant, was asked if he knew where his master had put a certain bundle containing stolen goods. He replied, "He came downstairs and I gave him a bit of black ribbon off my leg" (to tie up the bundle as there was no string to hand). Later, at the trial, he was questioned more closely about where the bag was put. He replied, "In a place in the parlour called 'a plant'." Q. "In what place was this plant?" A. "In the wainscot." Q. "Was it visible to anybody or was it a secret place?" A. "A secret place." Q. "How did the wainscot open?" A. There was a little hole at the bottom of it and one could put in a gimlet or the point of a knife and it lifted up and drew out." Q. "Was there a hinge to it?" A. "No."[113].

The stolen goods were removed from their hiding places in hackney coaches, little carts, by porters and even jackasses. The receivers also had their private furnaces in which to melt down plate, and coiners had moulds and presses for their work. Jewellery and

---

112. MAINWARING, pp. 89, 93-4.
113. OBSP, 1784-1785, p. 582.

trinkets were disposed of to pedlars at fairs, linen to hawkers and clothes to traders who came in from the country to buy stock[114]. The police were, in general, aware of where stolen goods were sold; as one hawker replied to an enquiring policeman, "I know nothing of it (the watch) only that it was sold for seven pounds ten ... you know as well as I do where we sell them"[115].

Until at least the beginning of the nineteenth century there was a certain difference between Christians and Jews in court cases, which later was no longer the case. In early times this is evidenced by the oft repeated "I am a Jew", "He is a Jew and so am I", "What are you?" "I am a Jew." "What else?" "I deal in old clothes," or "I am a Jew shoemaker," or "I am a constable, I am a Jew"[116].

It is not surprising, given the close and enclosed community, but of note nonetheless, that character witnesses in Jewish cases were almost always Jews (that is if the criteria of Jewish names is accepted). One exception was James Anderson, who when witnessing described Benjamin Benjamins as "of the ten tribes of Israel, the honestest". An astonished Judge asked if he himself was a Jew, to which he answered no, being a Scotsman by trade[117]. Other men seem to have earned their living by bailing people out and passing on the bail money for the next case. This became known, for obvious reasons, as "Jew Bail" and the magistrates appear irritated by the custom. One pedlar indignantly denied he bailed people for a living, and said he had only helped two friends that year!" "I hope," he said "if I have bailed a friend there is no reflection upon me for that"[118]. By the nineteenth century, prisoners no longer mention their religion. Such a catalogue of crimes must not be taken as an indication

114. MAINWARING, p.94.

115. OBSP, 1860-1861, p. 310.

116. OBSP, 1762-1764, p. 59; 1767-1768, p. 135; 1781-1782, p. 272.

117. OBSP, 1797-1798, p. 293. He may have meant he sold linen goods on credit as these men were known as "Scottish Drapers"; LIPMAN, 'Origins', in JHSE July 6, 1975.

118. OBSP, 1751-1755, p. 95.

of all-pervading criminality amongst the hawkers and pedlars. Certainly the greatest number were law-abiding, hard-working citizens as so many contemporary observers are quick to state. Apart from an innate honesty, inculcated by their religion, the harsh punishments for what would now seem comparatively small peccadilloes may also have reinforced the Jews' innate objection to taking part in criminal activities.

Old Satten Old Taffety or Velvet
Qui a des vieux Taffetas a vendre

4. Guildhall Library and Art Collection

5. Guildhall Library and Art Collection

Any old Clothes?

6. Guildhall Library and Art Collection

27

7. Guildhall Library and Art Collection

Any Old Cloaths.

8. Guildhall Library and Art Collection

CRIES OF LONDON.

Old Clo'—Old Clo'!

9. Guildhall Library and Art Collection

CHAPTER VI

ECONOMIC POSITION

It is difficult to estimate the economic position of the old clothes men, as existing statistics do not distinguish between them and other pedlars and hawkers.

The men traded on a very small capital and consequently could not earn very much. They made up for it by turning over their money quickly, selling in the afternoon what they had bought that day at whatever profit was to be had[1]. An author speaking of an old clothes man who came regularly to his street, said that his business must have been profitable, as he continued year after year[2]. Although the trade was in general far from lucrative, it could, and sometimes did, lead to better positions. Jews liked to better themselves and in spite of all their difficulties some of them managed to move up the ladder to a stall, or shop, and even on to a warehouse or manufacturing business. One or two families went from old clothes hawking to an empire of retail shops, but these were exceptions[3]. Quite a few old clothes men in seaports became ships' chandlers; the Navy list of 1814 gave 128 licensed agents with Jewish names[4].

The earning power of the men changed over the years. Up to 1820 or so there was a fairly good living to be had; for instance, a certain Mr. Lazarus "who dealt in old clothes about the street" met Moses Simmonds at a coffee house every day at three o'clock, and dined every evening with Benjamin Harris at six![5] One old foreign Jew who had begun by selling rhubarb, went on later to silks[6], and another sold sponges in the streets and was afterwards seen riding in

1. ATKINS, p. 60.
2. BENNETT, p. 39.
3. Mrs. Holston, personal communication.
4. Hyamson Collection, *Navy list to April 1814*, Navy Agents.
5. OBSP, 1819-1820, p. 92.
6. MAYHEW, *London*, vol. II, p. 46.

his own carriage[7]. This, in spite of Levi Nathan's remark, thirty years earlier, to a fellow hawker, "You are only an old clothes man and you know well that trade is very dead." But Levi had a great deal on his mind at the time, torn between his wife and children and the naughty Mrs. Parry, who flirted with other men before his very eyes in his own house[8].

By 1817 the houses in Rosemary Lane and a part of the Minories had become occupied by wholesale dealers, and cheap clothes were only to be found in the middle of the street[9]. One hawker said that around 1808 he could make as much as £5 a week by the purchase of old clothes in the streets, and that on average he earned £2 a week (a respectable sum in those days), but that now, thirty years later, old clothes men could only earn about £1 and sometimes not even that[10]. Another man said he bought and sold old clothes and mended boots, but all his efforts were in vain.

A collection of transcribed letters to the Treasury from hawkers in gaol owing to their inability to pay various fines, illustrates the depths of poverty among this class of people in the early nineteenth century. Mary Masterman, with three children and expecting another, said she received Parish Relief, "but that is so little that she knows not what to do with it when she receives it"[11]. And John Stallard, who had been a hawker since childhood and "until the present year had never been so far reduced as to be unable to pay a licence", had a wife, five children and suffered with rheumatism and "a dreadful bad leg"[12]. The wife of Lazarus Jacobs, who had eight children, had to sell all his goods and chattels to pay his fine and get him out of

7. C. KINGSLEY, (PARSON LOT pseud.), *Cheap Clothes and Nasty* (London, 1850).

8. NATHAN, p. 52.

9. HUGHSON, p. 15.

10. MAYHEW, *London*, vol. II, p. 308.

11. PROK, IR 51/5/p. 38.

12. PROK, IR 51/5, p. 12.

prison[13]. In general the petitioners seem to have been treated with some justice, their release from prison ordered and their fines either reduced, cancelled, or returned in part[14].

The situation gradually deteriorated and by 1848 the numbers of hawkers sheltered in asylums for the homeless poor, shot up, making the highest total over seventeen years of all occupations (one in every four individuals)[15]. By 1856 a social investigator classed hawkers as amongst the very poor, and examples of their homes as "one room, three school children"; "one room, five school children, one baby", or "hawker, two children, very poor," and so on[16]. Stallard (no relation to the hawker mentioned above) in 1876 noted that the cry of 'old clo' was less common than it used to be though an extensive business in wearing apparel was still carried on, but less profitably than formerly[17]. There was also a noticeable drop in the numbers of hawkers and old clothes men in criminal cases, though the reasons for this are unclear, possibly the anglicization of names masks their participation in crime. De Vega, in conversation with a Jew whom he met on his tour of the country, asked how it was possible that so many old clothes men could make a living from it. The reply was that it was a scanty one, and that many of them were half-starving and only undertook this kind of work because they were untrained in any other[18].

There are two opinions about the situation of country pedlars at this time which may have a bearing on those in towns. According to Alexander better communications by 1850 caused the rural trade to decline. But a policeman in 1891 remarked that "pedlars can only exercise their calling profitably in the country"[19]. I am

13. PROK, IR 51/5, p. 64.
14. PROK, IR 51/5, pp. 44, 39; IR 51/6, p. 57
15. MAYHEW, 'Survey', p. 67.
16. BOOTH, *Life*, vol. I, p. 37.
17. STALLARD, p. 9.
18. DE VEGA, vol. II, p. 77.
19. PROK, MEPO, 2/274.

inclined to agree with the latter view, that there may have been quite a good living to be made in and around country towns. As an example, an arrangement between a hawker called Isaac Johnson and Mr. McFadden, who lived in Lerwick in Shetland circa 1864, appears to have been quite profitable. Isaac employed men on a monthly basis to collect rags and other articles throughout the countryside, chiefly in exchange for stoneware at a fixed price, and he bought the rags at a fixed price too. The bags of rags were tagged and left at a farmer's house to be transported to Mr. McFadden in Lerwick, who was the stoneware merchant from whom Isaac bought his supplies. These two seem to have had close dealings as at one point McFadden lent Isaac the money to pay for his licence — "and entered it in the book." In spite of this, McFadden was not above doing private deals with one of Isaac's men, who had stolen one of Isaac's bags, and defended himself thus, "I do not think it necessary to enquiry where each lot of rags he purchases is procured — unless I notice new rope or other suspicious articles" — and then went on to inform Isaac that rumour suggested he was being robbed[20].

Other signs of profitable country hawking are to be seen in various wills, such as that drawn up in 1816 for Ceten Knight a hawker from Manstan Mortain, Bedfordshire. He left cottages and tenements with their appurtenances and other goods and chattels. Joseph Lemos also from Bedfordshire (died intestate), was a travelling hawker. His list of goods is considerable; the inventory contains a great variety and quantity of different goods:

	Velveteen and cords
42	pairs of hose
6	yards olive cloth
6	yards trousers cloth
2.5	yards trousers cloth
4	yards pocket linings
40	pairs worsted hose

20. Lerwick Archives (Shetland), 15th August 1864.

18	pairs black hose
9	grey and white hose
12	yards blind cotton
15.5	yards waistcoating
5	yards stout waistcoating
	Sundry remnants of printed cotton
	Sundry remnants of Union sheeting
4	yards thick black cloth
7	cotton waistcoats
9	pairs of trousers cord
16	handkerchiefs
5	yards black stuff
28	yards Saxony cloth
28	yards Orleans cloth
30	yards printed Seville cotton
5	yards printed calico
3	yards printed stuff
50	yards printed flannel[21].

One pedlar, also working in the country, arranged to take on an apprentice, "aged twelve or thereabouts", till he reached twenty-one. This "Poor child of the Parish" was "to faithfully serve in all lawful Business according to his Power, Wit and Ability, and honestly, orderly, and obediently in all things demean and behave himself during the said term". The pedlar had to "find, provide and allow unto said Apprentice competent and sufficient Meat, Drink, Apparel, Lodging, Washing and all other things necessary and fit for an Apprentice". He was also to be instructed and taught "in the art of the pedlar". The Parish seems most anxious that the child would no longer be or at any time become a charge on them, but did stipulate that at the end of his ten year term he was to receive "one new suit of clothes of all sorts fit and convenient for him." The indenture is legally made out on a printed form with added instructions in hand-writing,

21. Bedford, County Record Office, Wills.

121

signed by two church wardens and by two Justices of the Peace for the Apprentice, and also by the pedlar.[22]

It was common practice that Constables of Parishes were enjoined to make a return in writing to Justices of the Peace to present Poor children of the Parish who were suitable to be put out as Apprentices and to name persons/masters qualified to take them[23]. In 1784 there was a case in Inverness concerning John MacRae, a poor man "not worth a penny", a bark beater[24] who allowed his son to continue as a servant to the pedlar John MacKenzie, for a further three weeks till he could find a new servant to go into the Highlands in the West of Scotland. This was provided his mother agreed and that he was back in time for school. When the pedlar reappeared much later without his son, MacRae had him imprisoned in the local jail.

The pedlars' affidavit described how the boy was accused of stealing another pedlars' knife, which he had, in fact, found and sold for four pence. On being called by his master to be rebuked about the breakfast, he dashed out of the house, leaving his bonnet behind him in his hurry. He was heard to shout that "the devil take them if they ever saw him again". The pedlar anxiously sent two men to find him, but without success.

On being let out on bail the pedlar complained bitterly of being libelled "as if he had used the boy ill and it is even adventured to be said that the petitioner disposed of him as a slave to the West Indies, an allegiance as untrue as falsehood itself could devise". Further affidavits confirm his story and it is generally agreed in them that he treated MacRae more like a son than a servant. There is also mention of another boy "servant to John Sim, Chapman"[25].

22. Dorset Country Records Office, 22nd January? 1733.

23. Essex Country Records Office, D/P 18/10.

24. Bark was used in the making of a preservative for fishing nets. It may also have been used, to make rope.

25. Inverness, L/INV/BC 5/7/2 1748: Petition & Complaint of John Macrae, Letter from McKenzie from the Tolbooth, Letter from McKenzie on bail. Statement from John More.

There are several other instances of hawkers employing boys as servants, and in 1832 "a late servant of a hawker" applied for a licence on his own account [26].

In London, certainly, there was a sharp fall in fees from Pedlars' licences between 1882 and 1891 of 35 percent. Asked to give reasons for this, the different police stations gave different answers, one said it was due to distress among the pedlar class, as now their specialities were obtainable and sold as cheaply in shops. Another said hawkers were moving *out* of London owing either to the demolition of slum property, or the building over of open spaces where they had previously lived in caravans. However, this must have been balanced by the rise in immigrants moving in. A third said the selling of small articles was no longer profitable, and lastly, perhaps a more telling reason was that the police stations outside the Metropolitan area were less careful to whom they gave licences, and that they were known to be more tolerant towards men who spoke insufficient English. Also, licences were no longer required by men selling from barrows[27]. Now, too, as far as the old clothes men were concerned, there were sweated, cheap, machine-made clothes on the market so the poor could afford new, rather than second-hand goods.

From 1885 to 1893 in the lists of occupations, the hawkers appear amongst the lowest classes of "very poor". Recipients of relief (and Jews were always chary of asking for money from non-Jewish organisations, fearing the conversion of their children) were over 60 percent of all cases[28].

Whatever the reasons for the fall in profitability it was a real fact and grew steadily worse, so that by 1901 Jewish dealers in second-hand clothes became a rarity[29]. This is, in a sense, in contradiction of the fact that there was a greater flow of immigrants in

26. PROK, IR 51/6, p. 59.
27. PROK, MEPO, 2/274.
28. BPP, *Board of Trade Alien Immigration.* LXVIII p. 48.
29. *Church*, p. 350; OSTERLEY, p. 15; Mrs. Debina, personal communication.

the 80's. One can only suppose that many of these people went into the sweat shops and allied trades rather than into selling on the streets. By 1903 "throughout the East End there rises the same bitter cry, that the pauper alien has intensified tenfold the struggle for existence"[30]. Hard working and indomitable as they were, yet, as an old clothes man said of his kind, "they all die without money".

There is an interesting difference in the economic effects of the immigrant hawkers and pedlars in England and America. Coming from the same stock, in many cases from the same towns and villages in Germany, Russia and Poland, from the same class and with identical views and potentialities, yet the impression they made on the two economies differs radically.

In the British Isles the pedlars made no significant difference to the general economy, except, arguably, a passing depressing one on the poor of London, caused by their numbers. In America, on the contrary, there were two important results. The lesser, perhaps, was the part they took in the pioneering push into the middle and far West, where they accompanied the early pioneers into Indian territory, bringing much needed goods to the settlers, miners and even to the Indians themselves.

Linked to this, and of a greater importance to the economy, was the stimulation of the East coast factories, which produced the clothes, kitchen, farming and mining equipment needed by the pioneers and brought to them by the pedlars, and the consequent commencement of a well based expansion with lasting economic results.

Slight as the amount now appears, the charge for licences had an economic effect on the hawkers and pedlars downgrading their earnings. Licences for pedlars are mentioned as early as 1551, and these were the most important, and in many cases, the most onerous necessity for hawkers[31]. The Spanish-Portuguese

---

30. *Blackwoods Magazine* (Edinburgh, 1903), p. 132ff.
31. M. SPUFFORD, *The great reclothing of England* (London, 1984), pp. 6, 30.

Sephardic Synagogue was often called upon to help poor immigrants to pay their licences. In August 1837 Jacob Hadida, Baruch Duran, Israel Mendoza, David Bensusan, Mas(ao)d Benabu, Gab(rie)l Hen(rique)s de Souza, Isachor Levi and Jacob de Sol(omon) Hadida, all received 20/- towards hawkers licences[32]. The Licensing Board known as the Hawkers' and Pedlars' Office was appointed in 1697, the duty then being for one year[33]. In 1810 it was merged with the Hackney Coaches Board, attached to the Stamp Office, and in 1870 the licences were abolished and certificates (still spoken of as licences by both the hawkers and the police) were obtained from police stations. Hawkers with a horse continued to require licences until 1966 when the collection passed to county Councils[34].

A good deal of information can be found in the existing accounts of the Pedlars' and Hawkers' Office, submitted yearly to the treasury. In early times the money was used to pay for the transport involved in the "reduction of Ireland"[35].

The conclusions to be deduced from the numbers of licences taken out from 1740 to 1843 do not accurately indicate the actual numbers of hawkers, as it is well known that many hawkers either shared licences or omitted to take them out. In spite of this comparisons from one year to another can be made. Generally speaking the rises in numbers were gradual, though there are some high points. From 1740 to 1802 the numbers never rose above 1802 odd, and from then to 1840 they never fell below 1350 except for one year, and generally held above 2000, rising in 1837 to 8420. A study of the number of horse licences is also revealing. Until 1795 there were never more than 400 horse licences, but after that date the

32.   London, Spanish & Portuguese Synagogue Archives, Minute Books, August 1837. I should like to thank Miss Rodriguez-Pereira for kindly providing me with the information.
33.   PROK, AO1/1437, Roll, 40.
34.   PROCL, E/351, 1734, 1735.
35.   PROCL, E/351, 1735, 1737, 1739.

numbers of horses at one per pedlar increased steadily, reaching a peak of over 1000 by 1840.

Licences for two horses per pedlar increased from 1785, when there were one or two licences to a high point of nearly 2000 in 1810. Licences for three horses beginning in 1793 never rose above 70, except for the freak year of 1810, where 132 were taken out. The numbers of horse licences rose progressively with the number of foot licences[36].

The Hawkers' and Pedlars' Office was run by three commissioners who each earned £100 per year, a general Riding Surveyor at £200 and five other Riding Surveyors to cover ten miles outside London at £100 a year each. The latter were presumably so-called because they actually used horses to go about their work and were given extra money for their expenses and the upkeep of their horses[37]. These men were made redundant in 1832 and they were allowed compensation "for the loss of what should have been permanent employment". Inspectors, based all over the country, took their place[38].

Also employed were three London Surveyors at £50 each per year, and four clerks at the same pay, as well as a messenger at £30[39]. There was also a Mr. Ziggenhorne who had to make enquiries about the sufficiency of securities, and William Warrington, who made copies of papers for parliament.[40]

The staff was gradually increased. By 1741 there were nine riding surveyors and in 1781 Sarah Lewis appears as office keeper. She was paid £30 a year plus expenses for coal and candles[41].

36. PROK, AO1/1429 to 1453, Rolls 40 to 134.
37. PROCL, E/351, 1735.
38. PROK, AO1/1437, Roll 80. Hawkers' licences were stopped if they were sent to prison for other offenses, and these were never renewed thereafter.
39. PROCL, E/351, 1735.
40. PROCL, E/351, 1738.
41. PROK, AO1/1437, Roll 80.

Other office expenses included rent at £15 per annum, later to rise to £30 and disbursements for stationery. The articles listed under this heading were stamps for licences (at 2s each) and for bonds (at 12d), books, papers, copper plate printing systems, pens, ink, tape, wax, wafers and other wares[42]. They also on one occasion bought a press in which to place all these books and papers. Then there was office cleaning, seven and three quarters cauldrons of coals to heat the office, carriage and coach hire, and specifically coach hire to the tally court "thither and back", and also fees paid for tallying and parish duties. Interesting extras included money for New Year's gifts, and "food at the Treasury".

The penalties for forging a licence was £50 and £40 for lending or letting a licence or trading with a lent or borrowed one. This strict law does not seem to have had much effect, as in 1858 it was said the number of licences did not equal the number of hawkers, probably only one in five taking out a licence! Yet in 1876 Cheap Jack explained that before beginning to travel it was of the utmost importance to obtain a licence. As well as paying the usual fee, he had to get two vouchers from two respectable householders as well as the signature of the clergyman of the Parish as a guarantee of his respectability[43].

The hawkers and pedlars paid £4 a year for a foot licence, £8 for one horse, £12 for two horses and £16 for three, except for a short time from 1785 to 1788 when they were raised to £8, £16 and £24 respectively. There is one mention of a licence costing 50s (1820) but this may refer to the second payment, as they were allowed to pay in two parts[44]. The system appears rather elastic as the amount of the second payment varies from 8s to 40s. The men had to sign a bond for the second "moiety" and one supposes Mr. Ziggenhorne's enquiries related to the suitability of granting these[45]. A good many

---

42. PROCL, E/351, 1737.
43. HINDLEY, *Cheap*, p.2.
44. ALEXANDER, p. 66.
45. PROCL, E/351, 1735, 1736, 1737.

hawkers remained in arrears at the end of the year but if the second half was paid promptly a rebate of 2s to the pound was allowed. Because of the cost a good deal of trickery took place. Sometimes two of these pedlars showed the same licence and it is said they always knew where to borrow one if necessary[46]. After a certain time, the colour of the borders of the licence changed every year, probably to prevent more effectively the use of out of date ones[47].

Under certain circumstances a licence could be transferred, as in the case of a widow who transferred the six months remaining on her late husband's licence, to another hawker[48]. However, permission to recoup money on a licence in similar circumstances was sometimes refused[49], although a transfer from a deceased wife to her husband was accepted[50]. Licences were also sometimes "taken back" at the rate of £3.14s. each, in exchange for and in part duty on horse licences, the foot licence being returned and cancelled[51].

Four pounds was a great deal of money for the men to find, and as late as 1812 Joseph Harris had to save up for nine months to be able to buy one. As he travelled, meanwhile, without, he was in constant fear of being caught, and on one occasion he was arrested for being unable to produce a licence. Luckily for him, the Justice was away, so he got off with a five shilling fine and a promise never to peddle in that district again[52]. It was quite an escape, as in 1821 unlicensed pedlars were deemed "rogues and vagabonds" with dire consequences. Certainly the holders were proud of them. Solomon Isaacs, a character witness at a trial, remarked with some pride, "I travel with him (the accused) in the country, and have gone with a

46. DAVIS, p. 246.
47. Mr. Edgar Samuel, personal communication.
48. PROCL, E/351, 1739.
49. PROK, IR 51/6, p. 162.
50. PROK, IR 51/6, p. 168.
51. PROK, AO1/1433, AO/1761, Roll 60.
52. HARRIS, pp. 17-30.

licence these twelve years"[53]. And James Cohen's father was said to be "a very respectable man, a licensed hawker", the licence obviously being the proof of his respectability[54]. Further proof of their value is shown in the frequency with which they were stolen.

Licences were sometimes refused on the grounds that the pedlar in question knew too little English, however Michael Hart in 1830 had apparently no difficulty in obtaining a licence in his name, although he had been in England nine or ten weeks and spoke no English at all[55]. Other refusals depended on various circumstances, such as the case of "the notorious afternoon burglar", who was selling mats made by his wife, and was working under a false name. He was finally detected by the tattoo marks on his arms, and the police decided he should be refused renewal of his licence when the time came. They decided to leave him till then for fear of the newspapers getting hold of the case. He was what would now be called "a mugger"[56].

Army and Navy pensioners thought they had the right to hawk without a licence, but this was not so; the exceptions (Pedlars Act, 1810) was for freemen of towns or sellers of fruit, fish, eatables and drinkables[57]. Also exempted were hawkers of goods manufactured by themselves, as for example a hawker of Bonnet Boxes "of which he is the real maker". Further exemptions were for sellers of Acts of Parliament, Forms of Prayer, Proclamations, Gazettes, Licensed Almanacs, and other printed papers licensed by authority[58].

In 1785 hawkers living in a town could hawk there without a licence, but those who moved from fair to fair, market to market, or town to town required one. Moving from one district of

53. OBSP, 1738-1741 p. 362.
54. OBSP, 1898-1899, p. 569.
55. OBSP, 1830-1831, p. 971.
56. PROK, MEPO, 12/832.
57. FELIX, p. 15.
58. PROK, IR 51/6, pp. 59, 78.

London to another, was judged to be the same as moving to a different town[59]. Under a law of 1789 hawkers and pedlars had to have the words 'Licensed hawker' put on the most conspicuous part of every pack bag, trunk, case, cart or wagon in large legible Roman characters[60]. But this does not appear on any of the contemporary pictures which I have seen. However, Elkan Solomons recognised his empty box after it had been stolen by "the little plate on it where the licence was attached"[61]. There are many cases of hawkers being fined for not having the required words on their packs or carts. A hawker called Macpoland pleaded that "from the constant practice of placing my pack on the ground the proper mark was obliterated"[62].

It also appears that hawking was not allowed in any corporation under penalty of a £12 fine or committal to Bridewell (prison) for a certain time. In 1776 *The Gentleman's Magazine* recounts that a Jew had been charged for hawking hats in the city, and goes on to mention a case of a few years earlier, where John Stiles refused to pay the fine for hawking his goods in the City of London. Despite producing a hawkers' licence and his freedom of the city, Stiles was nevertheless committed to three months in prison[63].

It was said Jewish pedlars were withheld from the freedom of the city by jealous shop-keepers[64]. As Abraham Moses complains, "everyone knows we Jews are in the habit of asking more than we take, nobody ever expects to give what we ask. We are unfortunate fellows, the City authorities will not allow us to have a barrow in the street. I had only taken one shilling all day"[65].

59. PROK, MEPO, 537.
60. *Law of Hawkers and Pedlars* (London, 1822).
61. OBSP, 1847-1848 p. 519.
62. PROK, IR 51/5 1832 p. 24.
63. *GM*, vol. 37, p. 329.
64. Hughson, p. 541.
65. OBSP, 1860-1861, p. 94.

The licences' importance is described in a rather long and miserable set of verses in Hindley's *Cries of London* which sums up the situation as follows:

"To buy a new licence your money I crave
'Tis that which I want, & 'tis that which you have.[66]"

66. HINDLEY, *Cries*, p. 190.

CHAPTER VII

PERCEPTIONS

The perception by contemporary observers of immigrant Jews in general, and therefore of old clothes men and pedlars specifically, shows a kind of dichotomy. As always in such cases, prejudices, myths, differences in looks, dress and languages, influence judgment as well as, from time to time, the political and/or economic situation influenced their acceptance.

On the one hand there is, grudgingly sometimes, generously at others, admiration of the Jews' devotion to family and religious life, their sobriety, frugality, hard work and obedience to the law of the land, even their literacy and facility with languages. "Frugal to a fault, living on next to nothing, extremely industrious, patient and orderly" was one opinion expressed about them. Miss Machan, a 19th century parish worker, confirms this, describing the Jews as certainly free of immorality and drink and showing much greater industry and thrift than the local people[1]. "They are", says Hollingshead, "wonderfully independent and self-supporting, and keep up the ceremonies of their nation under the most adverse circumstances"[2]. One observer gives as his opinion, "Sir, Jews is better Christians than Christians themselves, for they help one another and we don't"[3].

On the other hand there was a kind of disgust at their appearance, "everything about them, their garb, their side curls and beards ... set them apart from their neighbours"[4]. Their sharpness, "Jews are tricky" according to Mayhew, their bargaining and persistence in making a sale, and amongst the old clothes men a love of gambling pushed to extremes,[5] were also resented.

1. BOOTH, *Notebooks*, XLVIII, p. 228; Clergy p. 100.
2. J. HOLLINGSHEAD, *Ragged London* (London, 1861), p. 48.
3. MAYHEW, *London*, vol. I, p. 442.
4. BERMANT, p. 123.
5. BOOTH, *Notebooks*, Local Government, Police & Publicans B.350, p. 189.

A more serious reproach was that they were dabbling in crimes, and were receivers of stolen property[6]. A further criticism, of Polish Jews in particular, was that they were liars who perjured themselves automatically[7]. This is confirmed by the Jews' defence pleas when on trial. In early cases in the 18th century, they begin "I am as innocent as the babe unborn" which changes later to "I know no more about it than a child",[8] and continues with flat denials of well-witnessed facts. Of course this could be due to their ignorance of the English language, but in general it appears to be their reaction to any claim against them, however well founded.

The difficulties of language and pronunciation influenced the way the English perceived the hawkers and pedlars, although this was not the case where Sephardic immigrants were concerned. Expressions such as "Buy a peddy lemon," or "Buy a vatch" are written under china figures and appear in printed caricatures, and also in many different versions of *The Cries of London*, a popular series of prints and in childrens' rhymes such as :

> "Old cloathes!
> Coats or preeches do you vant?
> Or puckles for your shoes?
> Vatches too me can supply
> Me monies von't refuse"[9].

A witness said "I took this to be his meaning — he speaking as most foreign Jews do, a sort of broken English"[10]. In another court case one witness referred to a man who "came to our shop ... on the 26th by the name of Jones, from his pronunciation I

6.   See above chapter on Crime.
7.   RUSSELL, p. 171.
8.   OBSP 1864-1865, p. 29.
9.   TUER, p. 77.
10. OBSP, 1756, p. 83.

said "You seem to be a Jew." He said "No I am not"[11]. Writing in 1806 the Reverend King said "If I may judge of her speech she was a Jewess"[12]. Cheap Jack mentions that several Jewish salesmen had a "peculiar spluttering" when calling their wares[13].

The mixture of Yiddish and English with a Polish or Russian inflexion, or perhaps a Scottish one, or Cockney infiltrated with Yiddish expressions, are a constant theme. Cheap Jack describes a discussion between a hawker and his customer, "Oh silber! Mr. Green, Levi knows, leave it to Levi, he knows silber in de dark by de feel"[14], and a Court interpreter says a prisoner speaks a patois with which he is well acquainted, a mixture of Hebrew and Polish — no doubt he means Yiddish. In the days when, generally speaking, only the rich travelled abroad, this mixture of tongues must have made a great impression on the lower classes and added to their irritation.

Some hawkers' knowledge of English was non-existent and they had to hold up their fingers when asked the price of an article. Some may never have learnt to speak or really understand it. Abraham Davis, when asked how he could identify a stolen watch, said "I have been in the business twelve years, I must know one watch from another, the name is altered (on the watch), there was another name. I cannot read English!"[15] Another old clothes man, Emmanuel Myers said in court that he could speak no English. Asked how he carried on his business, he replied, via an interpreter, that there were many people from his own country who helped him. "What do you do when there are none at home?" Myers answered "I generally make a motion", probably meaning he used sign language[16]. But there were also occasions when hawkers pretended ignorance of English to further their ploys, or avoid arrest.

11. OBSP 1773-1775, p. 365.
12. Mission, letter from J. Knight to Robert Winter, 24th December 1806.
13. HINDLEY, *Cheap*, p. 128.
14. HINDLEY, *Cheap*, p. 140.
15. OBSP, 1778, p. 17.
16. OBSP, 1783, p. 743.

Another cause of complaint against the Jews was noisiness and quarrelsomeness. The Rev. Alexander, who lived in Bethnal Green said that if only they would use their fists instead of their tongues, the quarrels would soon be over instead of keeping their neighbours up till midnight[17]. As late as 1850 a policemen was unable to make out what two quarrelling men were saying, partly because there was a great deal said —"there was no quieting them at all"[18].

The *Universal Songster* a collection of well known airs, published in three volumes in 1825, contains a fair proportion of songs about pedlars and old clothes men. These give an accurate, if exaggerated, picture of the way in which the English, probably the lower classes saw them[19]. The songs are in verse, but many are interspersed with monologues of the "patter" type, in heavily accented sometimes almost incomprehensible language. The Jew is seen as sharp, always ready to trick and cheat his customers, selling shoddy wares, yet a beguiling, sympathetic character, defiantly proud of being a Jew and one or two, at least, extol the singers' honesty. Some of the songs are pathetic:

> As throughout the week I roams
> A great distance from my home
> With my feet both wet and tired
> Still my goods they are admired
> Till some naughty little poys
> Who are out of good employs
> Cry out to me Jew Mayer, and folks stone on, etc.

17. BOOTH *Notebooks,* District 10, Bethnal Green East & Mile End Old Town East, Non-Conformist Churches, (183) p. 45.
18. OBSP, 1849, p. 17.
19. *Universal Songster*, p. 27ff.

or "Poor Little Mo", who,

> To get all vat I can and my customers try
> If I runs half a mile, never mind so dey buy
> Dey say no, off I go, mit my sweet meats and heart cakes
> Still I runs with my buns through the mud till my feet aches
> And dey think I'm all profid, but little dey know
> How ill and abused all day is poor little Mo.

or,

> My name is Nathan Solomon, clothes merchant and old rag
>   man
> I love sweet Becky Marks, her father is a bag man,

but poor Nathan has no luck as she loves another.

On a more cheerful note, there are "The Jolly Jew", "The Happy Jew", "De chinking of de cash", "The Honest Jew Pedlar". It seems Jews were generally considered ugly as one man was known as "the handsome Jew", obviously an unusual case[20]. Another song book from 1833 has a song about "Levi Lyon a good natured Jew", who says very appositely, "I can change, I can sell, I can buy, I can lend"— which about sums up the public's perception of the hawkers[21].

A late song from 1950 about a pedlar does not mention he is a Jew but the type of language would suggest this origin:-

> If you want this, I got
> If you want that, I got
> A coat and hat, I got
> Anything at all you want to buy
> People come to listen to my cry, etc[22].

20. OBSP, 1795-1796, p. 179.
21. *Richardson's New London Song Book* (London, 1833).
22. Mrs. Layson, personal communication; Johnny Pedlar's Song, c. 1950.

A *Cries of London* has a different view, speaking of an old clothes man,

> "A Jew may have a heart as pure
> As any Christian I am sure".[23]

    The attitude of shopkeepers to hawkers varied from a reluctant acceptance to latent or open hostility[24]. Their chief complaint voiced in many broadsides addressed to Parliament from 1674 onwards, was that the itinerants were free of taxes which they had to pay and that most of them paid neither Scot nor Lot, Taxes, Rent or any other charge[25]. In fact the country hawkers did have to pay market tolls, though this varied from place to place and time to time. John Bebbington speaks of waiting in momentary dread of the Bellman coming for his toll, "which must be paid no matter how or when you get it"[26]. The shopkeepers also complained that the pedlars sold false goods, "not fully burnt earthenware and glass not well nealed but cracked and faulty". This was a foretaste of what was to come; later it was said their knives, scissors, and razors were made to sell, but not to cut or shave[27]. Further, the pedlars, rather cheekily, offered their goods to the shops' customers at their very doors, and even called them out of the shops with offers to sell the same goods at lower prices.

    These complaints continued with added groans about their dishonesty, and even that they did not have to keep up a good reputation as they frequently changed their walks; in spite of the shopkeepers' efforts to get the itinerant trade abolished, this was continually refused, and a few voices even spoke up for the pedlars.

23. Old Clothes Man, etching by Busby in *Cries of London*, 1823.

24. ALEXANDER, p. 69.

25. Guildhall Library, Broadsides, B.1675, B.1692, B. 1693, B.1697 12.59), B.1691 (12.71 s.12.66).

26. BEBBINGTON, Folio, J. 377.

27. BUSBY.

11

A broadside about 1690 lists six cogent reasons for their non-suppression and another in 1860 from "a friend of the friendless" defends them against allegations of obstruction and accuses the police of brutality towards them[28].

Shopkeepers, when they asked for hawkers to be removed, found that clients preferred streets where they were to be found, and consequently lost custom. At all events the pedlars were, in practice, rarely moved by the police of London, so the shopkeepers began to put stalls outside their shops to prevent the establishment of some hawker or other. The people who lived in Cutler street put stalls not only on the pavement outside their doors, but in the road too, and they let them out for threepence or sixpence a day[29].

Jewish shopkeepers were disliked by their Gentile neighbours, the old clothes shops in Holywell Street had very persistent proprietors who were "strikingly visible and highly vocal"[30]. They often came out into the street, seized potential customers by the arm and more or less led them into their shops[31]: "their very great importunity is often troublesome to the object of it"[32].

De Vega, an eccentric Englishman, who dressed up as a Spaniard and set off on a tour of England, supporting himself by singing to the accompaniment of a guitar, said they were very polite whilst forcing him into their shops. He was able to buy just what he needed for his tour, including a brown cloak lined with green baize and a striped waistcoat, which he told the owner to shake well![33] *The Gentleman's Magazine* disapproved of "amateur mendicants" like De

28. Guildhall Library, Broadsides, 1860 (8.30).
29. OBSP, 1840, p. 665.
30. ENDELMAN, p. 182.
31. AUSTIN, p. 67.
32. *Expositor*, vol.IV, p. 185.
33. DE VEGA, vol I, p. 14.

Vega, as they considered it unfair to real beggars, but added that he did give £69 of his receipts to charity[34].

There seems to have been even greater hostility between English costers and Jewish hawkers, the former saying Jews grabbed pitches which had been theirs for many years, and that they did business for unfairly long hours, and undercut by cheap selling[35]. An ex-president of the costers' federation complained of *all* foreigners who "decline to recognize the sanctity of the pitch, but will rise at dawn to oust an old occupant who has worked up a connexion" and "insist on staying in prohibited places which brings down the authorities on everyones' heads"[36]. This was repeated by an observer who described Jews as deficient in social morality, who although they pay their debts and keep their contracts, were "unchecked by the feelings of class loyalty and trade integrity"[37]. In short, "Well, about these 'ere Jews, wot I sez is this, they're a dirty lot, I 'ates 'em; they works all day and 'arf the night, and as to wittles they eats 'ardly nofink, 'arf a 'erring 'll larst a 'ole family more nore a week"[38]. Of such, myths are made. This is the uneducated view, but it is underwritten in the late 19th century by literature of an anti-alien, anti-semitic nature, thinly-veiled as serious books on social questions, such as those written by Evans-Gordon, Arnold White and Colin Nicholson.

It does seem more than a little unfair to criticize these newcomers, who scarcely spoke a word of English, or knew anything of local conventions, for not abiding by unwritten laws which were probably incomprehensible to them. On the other hand, it must be admitted that the old clothes men and the urban pedlars, partially by their numbers and generally by their persistence, made a nuisance of themselves. Gartner says the costers and tradesmen constituted the

34. *GM*, July 1830, p. 239.
35. GARTNER, pp. 60, 61.
36. *Blackwoods Magazine* (Edinburgh, 1903), p. 132.
37. BOOTH, *Life* p. 189.
38. *Church*, vol.1-3, 1896, p. 190.

most bitterly anti-alien group in London, but some workmen were also in this category.

The old clothes man in earlier periods *was* often beaten and ill-treated, more so when popular feeling rose against the Jews at the time of the proposed Naturalization Bill. This was a Bill which would have allowed Jews who had lived in England for three years, to be naturalized, without having to take the Sacrament. The Bill passed but was repealed.

Jews felt obliged to stay indoors for some time after the "Chelsea Murder" in 1771, when a gang of Jews killed a man during a burglary. It is significant that the Recorder prefaced their sentence with a judicious compliment to the principal Jews ... "and hoped no person would ignorantly stigmatize a whole nation for the villainous few, whom they had done everything they consistently could, to bring to punishment"[39]. According to Francis Place speaking of the 18th century, it was thought good sport to maltreat Jews, and they were ill-used even in the principal streets. They were hooted, kicked, cuffed and had their beards pulled and spat on without any protection from the passers-by, or the police. "Dogs", he said, "would not be permitted to be treated in the way Jews were"[40]. An eighteenth century children's book admonished children thus: "Some foolish children delight in making sport of them (i.e. old clothes men) but it is a very cruel and idle practice[41]. One poor old hawker was set upon by two men who took two shillings from him. A witness who saw the men attack him, did tell them it was a shame to treat an old man so[42].

Jewish hawkers were also sometimes accused unjustly. A case, said to have taken place in Guernsey, involved a murder and an attempt was made to implicate "Levi the Jew, whom you all know, who has travelled these islands for twenty years." Even if this story is a Victorian fiction, it is significant that a Jewish pedlar appears as a

39. *GM*, 1771, p. 56.
40. BESANT, p. 262, quoting Francis Place.
41. *Cries of London* (London, 1790), Manuscript.
42. OBSP, 1783, p. 743.

likely murderer[43]. Bina Levy indicted with Isaac Solomon for stealing a silver tankard, said in her defence, "It is a public house, where one goes and another comes and they put it upon us because we are Jews"[44]. A prisoner said he was afraid of getting his brains knocked out because the mob had hold of him and accused him of being a Jew, "so I was afraid to speak"[45]. The Jews began to hit back at their assailants towards the end of the 18th century. In 1783 Mendoza, a Jewish prize fighter, became the idol of young Jews who took to boxing in emulation of him. The manner in which they were treated changed as a consequence[46]. Contemporary prints begin to show previously undreamt of scenes, such as an old clothes man punching an assailant who tried to pull his beard. A certain Huke asked the young Mendoza rather nervously, "Do you want to fight me in earnest? I know you, and you may be as good a man as your father for all I know"[47].

In spite of this the old clothes men still suffered some harassment. As late as 1802 Lyon Abrahams went into a pub, put his bag of clothes and was promptly "skylarked" (i.e. teasing akin to bullying) by the attendant company[48]. And on another, later, occasion the hawker, Mordecai Jacobs, was indicted for stealing a pair of shoes. He explained that Hodson offered him shoes for 6s. Mordecai said "4s." and agreed on 5s. He put them in his bag and paid up, but Hodson ran after him down the mews and threatened to charge him if he didn't give him 6s. — "because I was a Jew"[49]. However, urban hawkers and pedlars never had to face the grave dangers of country pedlars.

43. *The Universal Magazine* (London, 1726), vol. 80, p. 205.
44. OBSP, 1760-1762, p. 113.
45. OBSP, 1762-1764, p. 135.
46. BESANT, p. 177.
47. OBSP, 1818-1819, p. 425.
48. OBSP, 1802, p. 235.
49. OBSP, 1825, 1826, p. 398.

Early 20th century old clothes men are remembered now with affection by people who were then East End children[50]. They used to give children jam jars in return for rags, very useful for tiddlers or worms when going fishing, or sometimes a cup and saucer or a windmill on a stick[51]. If a child brought in a good amount of rags or clothes, he might be given a goldfish in a bowl. Bundles of newspapers were also required and naughty boys damped them or put a brick in the middle of the bundles, because they were paid by weight. If they were discovered the hawkers used to chase them and cuff them if they were caught.

One old clothes man had a roundabout on his cart with fourteen chairs which was worked by manually turning the handle. He gave free rides for clothes, cups and saucers, or jam jars. He hung the sacks of cloth on meat hooks from railings round the cart, or else stacked them underneath it. A taxi-driver kindly drew a sketch of the roundabout for me, which he said had a circular enclosed seat fixed onto a central drum. It was reached by a small ladder at the back and the door at the top of the steps had a seat fixed to it to complete the circle. The drum turned on a ratchet system worked by hand. The cart was decorated with flags on the enclosing iron-work[52]. When the hawkers' carts were standing for any length of time during the summer months, they covered the wheels with wet sacks to prevent the wood cracking[53]. Many of the carts were decorated with brightly coloured paintings of roses and other flowers and designs[54].

It is astonishing to find quite a number of people who remember the roundabout man, perhaps because it was one of the ingredients in what appears to have been, despite its poverty, a very happy childhood, in which the old clothes man, like his counterpart the country pedlar was a familiar and useful central figure.

50. Taxis Nos. 3, 5, 1.
51. Taxi No. 6.
52. Taxi No. 10.
53. Taxi No. 11.
54. Mrs. Camilleri, personal communication.

Their disappearance was a gradual process due to various factors but mainly to the invention of the sewing machine and the consequent arrival on the market of new, cheap, clothes from the sweat shops, which were preferred to second-hand ones[55]. Yet, the old clothes men continued to exist up to the last war, and even later up to 1950, in the remoter areas of the British Isles, still plying their trade in the old manner, an archaic reminder of their erstwhile usefulness.

55. Mr. Edgar Samuel, personal communication.

APPENDIX

Pedlars Wares

A.   Artificial flowers.

B.   Buckles, white metal, carved silver, crystal etc. Buttons (Bristol Stone) Buttons, Strings of bracelets, Breastpins, Bed linen, Brooches, Basins, Braiding , Braces, Bodkins, Burning glass, Brushes, Barometers, Binding, Breast Buckles set with pearls, or garnets, Bachelors Buttons.

C.   Cigars, Cuckoo clocks, Clasps (silver) Combs, Cutlery, Cheese grater, Candlesticks, Candle snuffer (scissor type, dunce-cap type), Cony skins, Cobweb lawn, Crosses, Curtain hooks, Coral beads, Coach glasses, Crepe shawls, various types of cloth.

D.   Driving whip.

E.   Extinguisher (double japanned), Ear rings, Ewer.

F.   Figurines (plaster), Frying pan.

G.   Gold leaf (from uniforms), Gaming boards, Griddle,Ginger.

H.   Hosiery, Haberdashery, Head (for a cane) silver and ditto pinchbeck, Handsaw, Hardware, Harness, Handkerchiefs.

I.   Isinglass.

J.   Jewelry (cheap) and (better type).

K.   Knives (many bladed), Pocket knives.

L.   Lace, Linen drapery, Lemons, Lockets, Lancets, Leather pocket books.

M.   Multiplying glass, Microscopes, Musical Boxes, Mace, Millinery.

N.   Needles, Nibs, (flexible with holder), Necklaces. Sail needles.

O.   Oranges, Ostrich feathers, Otto of Roses.

P.   Pins, Pens, Pencils, Paper, Pin cushions, Pocket mirrors, Penknives, Prints (re: King and Queen, Four Seasons, Cardinal virtues, Recent naval victory, Pilate, Prodigal

Son, Nativity, Crucifixion, Paul, Obscene pictures), Plates, Poker, Pepper, Points, Purses, Pencil cases, Plush covers.

Q.   Quills.

R.   Rings (gold) Razors, Rhubarb, Ribbons.

S.   Spectacles, Slippers, Sealing wax, Shaving boxes, Sponges, Sheets of songs, Steel pins, Saddles, Soup ladle, Salt cellars (cut glass flint), Straps, Shaving pastes, Snuff boxes (silver, japan), Scent boxes (japan), Scissors, Silk satins, Seals, Shells, Strops, Strainer, Silk pieces, Shoe buckles, Stock buckles, Shew glass, Saddle cloths.

T.   Trinkets, Tea-Tongs (silver), Thimbles, Toys (French and Dutch), Toilet articles, Tobacco, Trifles of tin and wire. Tape, Tea strainers, Thermometers, Telescopes.

V.   Vase.

W.   Watches, weather glasses, Watch chain (silver, pinchbeck), Writing paper (Bath Post), Wafers, Warming pan, Wedding rings.

INDEX

England 13-6, 27, 29, 31,
  35, 39, 44, 57, 59, 65,
  81-2, 88, 95, 98-9, 104-6,
  124, 129, 138, 140
engravings 55, 61, 62, 79
epidemic 18
Eskdale Muir 37
Evans-Gordon 139
Exeter 22
factories 75, 124
fairs 22, 25, 33, 35, 55,
  57-8, 115
Falkirk 24
Falmouth 36, 63
Falmouth, Zender 30
families 19, 31, 57, 59,
  68-9, 103, 117
farming 21, 124
fashion 46, 50, 62-3, 87, 99
Fasts 56
Fents 75
Festivals 55-7
fever 34
Fielding, *Sir* John 105
Fife 24
fines 58, 118-9
fish 64, 66, 129
Fitzroy Square 79
flannel 121
Foley, Russel 28
food 20-1, 26, 35, 66, 81,
  90, 127
forgery 113
forks 112
Fort George 24
France 15, 17, 39, 51, 81,
  98
Franks, Mr. 38
Free Market 22
fruit 18, 26, 129

Gabrial, Solomon 109
gambling 61, 86-7, 96,
  107, 132
garments 16, 67, 85
Gartner, L. 139
Gentiles 60
The Gentleman and Porter
  51
The Gentleman's Magazine
  19, 74, 130, 138
The George 108
George III 57
German 13, 30, 55, 59,
  64, 99
Germany 22, 37, 98-9, 105,
  124
Gershon, Henry 101
Gerson, George 35
ghettoes 16, 102
ginger 41, 45, 144
Glasgow 13, 22, 24, 37,
  46, 78
glass 42, 69-70, 101-2,
  106, 109, 137, 144-5
gold 24, 36, 38-9, 43,
  52-4, 61, 69, 70, 96,
  110, 144-5
Goldsmith, Henry 111
Goose Fair 25
Government House 39
Gravesend 22
Great Synagogue, London
  37, 105
Greenwich 62
guilds 14
guineas 14-5, 29, 36,
  38-40, 106
gun 44, 95
hackney 51, 53, 56, 69, 74,
  114, 125

Index

Isaacs, Solomon 128
isinglass 41, 144
Isles of Scilly 17-8, 32, 47, 53
Israel, Isaac 111
Israel, Isaiah 107
Israel, Sarah 70
Italians 32
jackasses 114
jackets 87
Jackson, Edward 36
Jacob, Garrulous 109
Jacobs, James 112
Jacobs, Lazarus 81, 118
Jacobs, Mary 40
Jacobs, Mordecai 71, 106, 141
Jacobs, Moses 66
jail 122
jam jars 142
Jerusalem pony 27
Jessel, Harry 64
Jew Bail 115
The Jeweller's Arms 53, 65
jewellery 24, 30, 37, 41, 44, 50, 53-4, 114
Jewish Association for the Protection of Women 97
Jewish Chronicle 47, 57, 59, 61, 101
Jewish Community 15, 23, 106
Jewish Congregation 20, 30-1, 63-4
Jewish Industrial School 113
Jewish Legal Council 100
Jewish Museum 46, 52
Jewish Poor 15-6, 23, 101

Johnson, Isaac 120
Joseph, Henry 42
Judah, Isaac 106
Justices of the Peace 29, 77-8, 122
Kent 40
Kerseymere 89
kettles 54
killed 36-7, 140
Kimhi, Jacob 44-5, 48, 99
King, *Reverend* 29, 47, 60, 97, 134
The King's Head and Rose 65
Kingsmen 103
knives 15, 114, 122
Knight, Ceten 120
Kosher 29, 66, 102
Kybeck 66
laces 20-1, 45, 53, 80
ladders 28, 109, 117, 142
ladles 52
Lanark 24
Landberg, Kirsh 50
language 19, 98-9, 132-6
lantern 95
lavender 54
law 13, 28, 42, 56-7, 63-4, 66, 73, 78, 81, 84, 95, 98, 104, 112, 116, 121, 127, 130, 132, 139
Lazarus, Mr. 117
Lazarus, Aaron 107
Lazarus, Henry 73-4
Leadenhall Street 59
leather 21, 26, 37, 49, 50, 52, 57, 103, 110, 144
Leicester 78, 100
lemons 41, 44, 47, 93, 133, 144

12

Missionary Society 101
money *passim*
Monmouth Street 77, 90, 92, 108
Moorfields 92
Mordecai, Elias 106, 109
Morning Post 47
Moroccan 61
Morpeth (Northumberland) 21
Morris 108
Moses, Abraham 130
Moses, Henry 30
Moses, Hyman 66, 111
Moss, Peter 112
moulds 114
muffs 61, 87
murders 18, 28, 35-6, 104-5, 140-1
Myers 55, 69
Myers, Emmanuel 134
Nathan, Abraham 114
Nathan, Levi 15, 17, 51, 66, 78, 85, 98, 118
Nathan Solomon 23
Naturalization Bill 104, 140
Navy 39, 117, 129
necklaces 44, 53, 144
needles 21, 43, 53, 144
neighbourhoods 18, 33, 60, 65, 77, 81, 83, 91
New Christians 13
Newcastle 22, 37, 72
Newton 31
Nicholson, Colin 139
North African 45-6
North Kensington 75
Northumberland 21
Norwich 27
Nottingham Goose Fair 25
nutmeg 41
nuts 64, 93
oilskin 53
old clothes *passim*
Old Clothes Exchange 79, 82
old livery 69
Old Sammy 22, 32, 40, 52
Oppenheimer, Samuel Wolf 81
oranges 47
ornaments 69
pans 54
Paris 81, 100
----- Sanhedrin 100
Parishes 40, 73, 77-8, 97, 118, 121-2, 127, 132
Parkgate 31
Parliament 81, 126, 129, 137;
Acts of 16, 28, 129
Parry, Mrs. 15, 85, 98-9, 118
passport 81
Patrol House 95
pavements 91, 93, 138
pawnbrokers 90, 108, 112
The Pawnbrokers Gazette 112
Payne, Jayne 70
pearls 36-7, 50, 110, 114
pease 108
pedlar *passim*
Pedlars Act 129
Pedlars' Draught 19, 20, 37, 41, 50, 55, 58, 99, 122-3, 125-6
pencils 14, 41-2, 53, 144

penknives 42, 144
pens 34, 127, 144
pensioners 85-6, 129
pepper 45, 52, 145
Persia 80
petitions 77-8, 104, 122
Petticoat Lane 59, 71, 79,
  80, 84, 91, 94
pewter 111
Philips, John 82
Phillips Buildings 18, 54,
  79, 83, 104, 111
Phillips, Gadaliah 111
Phillips, Joseph 83
pickles 41, 51
pickpocketing 84, 110
Pie powder 58
pies 54
pig wife 71
Pincas, Moses 37
pins 45, 50, 52-3, 144-5
Place Francis 140
playing cards 55
ploys 134
Plymouth Congregation 64
Plymstock 36
pocket-knives 53
Polack, Isaac 15
Poland 16, 22, 124
police 24, 45, 48, 73-4, 77,
  93, 95, 101, 103, 111-3,
  115, 119, 122-3, 125,
  129, 132, 135, 138, 140
Polish 13, 50, 55, 63, 86,
  133-4
pony 24, 27-8
poor *passim*
porcelain 52, 63
Porter, Edward 23
Portsea 22

Portsmouth 22, 39
Portuguese 13, 38, 57, 59,
  64, 98, 124-5
post shay 29
pots 21, 52, 109, 111
prejudice 60, 132
Price, William 36
prices 75, 103, 137
Princess of Wales 37, 57
prison 69, 82, 106, 108,
  115, 119, 126, 130, 134,
  141
proprietors 31, 89, 92, 95,
  138
prostitution 97
public coaches 56
public houses 19, 26, 31-3,
  47, 53, 56-8, 65-6, 75,
  78, 84-5, 89, 100-1, 106,
  108-9, 111, 141
Public Offices 56
pullovers 47, 54
purses 37, 46, 84, 145
Rabbis 13, 20, 56-7, 67,
  97-8
Rabbi Jonathan 98
Rabbi Stern 97
Rabbinovitz, Joel 19
races 60
Rag Fair 77, 81, 84-5, 94,
  107
rags *passim*
rail 25, 48
rain 34-5, 81, 88
razors 15, 137, 145
Receivers 103-5, 112-4,
  133
Regent's Canal 89
religious 13, 45, 57, 64,
  66, 98, 100, 132

Index

Index